Economic and Environmental Cost of Traffic Congestion in India

This book explores one of the most prevailing problems of the contemporary urban world, i.e., traffic congestion and its economic, environmental, and health implications.

Generally viewed as an urban menace, the problem of traffic congestion has huge economic implications, which are often overlooked by urban planners. This book examines and quantifies the costs and adverse consequences of traffic congestion, which include emissions, loss of productive hours, fuel wastage, and the adverse effects on the health of commuters, among others. It provides a comprehensive and scientific understanding of the underlying problems of traffic gridlocks by analyzing empirical evidence and data from Bengaluru, a city in South India. It also offers solutions and highlights innovative measures that draw from both economic and engineering perspectives to counter and reduce the tangible and intangible costs of traffic congestion.

This book will be of interest to both academic and non-academic readers of economics, environmental economics and econometrics, transport economics, urban planning, transport geography, as well as planners and policy makers.

Vijayalakshmi S is Research Associate at the Centre for Economic Studies and Policy at the Institute for Social and Economic Change, Bengaluru, India.

Krishna Raj is Professor at the Centre for Economic Studies and Policy (CESP) at the Institute for Social and Economic Change, Bengaluru, India

Economic and Environmental Cost of Traffic Congestion in India

Vijayalakshmi S and Krishna Raj

Routledge
Taylor & Francis Group
LONDON AND NEW YORK

First published 2024
by Routledge
4 Park Square, Milton Park, Abingdon, Oxon OX14 4RN

and by Routledge
605 Third Avenue, New York, NY 10158

Routledge is an imprint of the Taylor & Francis Group, an informa business

British Library Cataloguing-in-Publication Data
A catalogue record for this book is available from the British Library

ISBN: 978-1-032-66493-4 (hbk)
ISBN: 978-1-032-66228-2 (pbk)
ISBN: 978-1-032-66229-9 (ebk)

DOI: 10.4324/9781032662299

Typeset in Sabon
by Deanta Global Publishing Services, Chennai, India

Contents

Figures

Tables

Foreword

It is a pleasant privilege for me to write a Foreword to this interesting book by S Vijayalakshmi and Krishna Raj on the *Economic Cost of Traffic Congestion in Bengaluru*. It is based on the PhD thesis by the first author prepared under the perceptive and able guidance of the second author. The book is a significant original contribution to the literature on environmental economics, both from academic and policy angles. It is written with care and competence on an important contemporary problem affecting day-to-day life in our cities.

Human impact on environment, especially climate change, has by now overtaken the impact due to natural factors. In fact, human impact itself is interacting with natural factors in such a way as to aggravate the impact of the latter. Environmental problems due to human intervention started in a noticeable way in the world right from the beginning of the Industrial Revolution in the eighteenth century. Soon they caught the attention of poets, novelists, activists, public thinkers, and philosophers in the nineteenth century itself. John Keats, William Blake, and William Wordsworth were the prominent poets who expressed their unhappiness with the effects of the Industrial Revolution. Charlotte Bronte, Elizabeth Gaskell, and Charles Dickens were among the prominent novelists who graphically described the living and working conditions of industrial labour.[1] Among the main public thinkers of the nineteenth century, included now among social scientists, who critically analyzed the impact of the Industrial Revolution, were Thomas Malthus, Friedrich Engels, Karl Marx, and Henry David Thoreau. Though the negative impacts on nature and landscape from an aesthetic angle were emphasized by poets, the horrible exploitation of industrial labour, prevalence of child labour, the poor nutritional status of industrial workers, and their dangerous working conditions were highlighted by novelists and public thinkers. Smoke and air pollution, in general, pollution of streams, and devastation of the landscape did receive attention, but the impact on human beings was the main focus of these thinkers. Industrial development thus had tremendous costs, which were not borne by the producers or industrialists but were imposed on others and could not just be ignored.

It naturally fell to the lot of economists to take due note of such costs, first in theory and then in terms of actually estimating them. Economics, being a young and evolving science then, it took quite some time for it to do it. I think A C Pigou was the first economist who formally began the process by distinguishing between Social and Private Net Products in his seminal book, *The Economics of Welfare*, published first in 1920 in London by Macmillan (pp.183–196). To reduce or balance the divergence between social and private net products, Pigou even suggested government intervention in the form of 'bounties' or 'taxes' as suitable, leading him to the concept of a tax on pollution, which played an important role in environmental policy. This led to the development of the concept of 'positive' and 'negative' 'externalities', the former deserving encouragement or 'bounties' and the latter deserving taxes. The next important landmark was the publication of an outstanding article, 'The Problem of Social Cost', by R H Coase in *The Journal of Law and Economics*, in 1960. The next step in theoretical development was to go beyond a single or individual polluting factory and its victims who bear the costs or negative externalities and view costs of economic growth as a whole. A significant contribution in this regard came from *The Costs of Economic Growth* by E J Mishan in 1967.

Numerous publications of books and articles have come out subsequently, contributing to the development of Environmental or Ecological Economics as a scientific discipline in its own right. As environmental problems aggravated, publications have also kept pace with them. As a result, awareness of these problems, particularly of climate change and its consequences, has also improved, and policy instruments have been honed up. Sadly, however, this is not reflected in the will to sincerely solve them both on the part of the state and the public at large. This is because the focus has been almost wholly on technological solutions and avoids the real problem – our increasingly extravagant and anti-environment lifestyle. Technological innovations are no doubt needed, but they alone cannot solve the problem. Take the example of a cardiac disease. A cardiologist or a cardiac surgeon is a super technologist, who can not only perform various tests to make an accurate diagnosis but also use surgical procedures to cure the disease. But when a cardiac patient approaches him (or her), the cardiologist also advises a change in the lifestyle and not just medicines and surgery. The patient is advised to restrict diet, avoid fats, exercise and meditate regularly, relax, and so on. In solving environmental problems also, a change in lifestyle is necessary along with technological solutions. But this is hardly done. We have the genius for technological innovations but not the strength of will to mend our behaviour to make it eco-friendly and sustainable.

> Of what wonder is the human species!
> Of intriguing mind, hard to decipher!

The best in cleverness of intellect, yet
the worst in benignity of behaviour![2]

But we cannot afford to give up in despair, as our very future – the future of human species – is at stake. We have to continue to expose environmental problems faced by us, analyze them, and find solutions. In this context, the present research study by Vijayalakshmi and Krishna Raj is most welcome and pertinent. It quantifies economic and environmental costs of traffic congestion in Bengaluru. In an economist's perspective, these costs are viewed as negative externalities imposed by vehicle users on other users. The direct economic impact of traffic congestion consists first of the opportunity cost of time stuck in traffic congestion ('time delay') as a productivity loss and second of the cost of additional fuel used as a result of traffic congestion. The environmental impact is a cost measured in terms of expenses on meeting health problems caused by prolonged exposure to air pollution and the loss of productivity as a result of ill health caused thereby. These 'environmental' costs have also economic dimensions. The study is conducted for Bengaluru as the case. This is a city which has gained international notoriety for its traffic jams. The time taken to cover a given distance has been increasing exponentially over the last decades. Bengaluru has the second-highest motorization rate (the number of vehicles per 1,000 persons) in the country – 441 as compared with 443 in New Delhi. The study says that on an average, the commuters in Bengaluru are stuck for 38 minutes every day in traffic congestion. But apart from traffic congestion due to being stuck at a spot, there is also an impact on the speed of traffic movement even when it is not so stuck. The vehicles sometimes literally move an inch by inch, with the distance between two vehicles dropping to just about a foot sometimes! This sharp drop in speed also has economic and environmental costs specified above. Additionally, it causes road rages, sometimes resulting in hand-to-hand fights and even murder! Such incidents also cause traffic congestions away from signals. The psychological impact of such incidents can be inestimably high!

The study estimates that the total economic cost of traffic congestion in Bengaluru amounts to 0.58 per cent of the city's GDP. It may appear to be a small and sustainable proportion. But this is misleading, as the estimate includes only the cost of additional fuel use and the opportunity cost of time wasted due to traffic congestion and excludes the cost in terms of adverse impact on health and its impact, in turn, on productivity. This exclusion makes a huge difference. Though the study has duly estimated health and productivity costs of traffic congestion, it has stopped short of expressing them as a proportion to the city's GDP as done in the case of the two economic costs, maybe due to some technical difficulty. Apart from these economic and environmental costs, the impact of increased air pollution on global warming is also to be taken into account. According to a UN Report on Climate Change, motor vehicles account for virtually all of the carbon monoxide and lead in the air of cities and a major portion of NOx and toxic chemicals. Of course, this is not due to traffic congestion specially, but it surely aggravates the problem. I am not making these observations in criticism of the present book as such, – they are not meant to detract from its significance or merit but to only caution against economists making quick judgements of the environmental costs being low in comparison with GDP. There is a grave risk that they may be significantly underestimated. Take the example of impact of air pollution on mortality rate. How do you put a price tag on human life? Air pollution is estimated to cause seven million premature deaths every year in the world.[3] Health costs may be estimated by taking note of expenses on medicines and treatment, and productivity loss due to days lost in illness. But what about distress and trauma suffered due to illness, and adverse impact on health which may last much longer than the apparent disease? Prolonged and regular exposure to air pollution is feared to damage lungs, heart, and brain.

Apart from estimating the economic and environmental costs of traffic congestion, the book has some very interesting findings to report. The main cause behind traffic congestion is the phenomenal increase in private vehicles, which in turn are caused by equally phenomenal increase in the incomes of the middle class. The commuters are rapidly shifting from public to private transport. However, the study finds that women tend to prefer public transport more than men. The study is critical of policy makers to solve the problem mainly from the supply side by increasing road network, construction of flyovers, etc. The solution lies in making public transport more attractive and discouraging private transport. The experience of operating Metro lines has shown encouraging results, as the study shows. It also finds that bus fares in Bengaluru are comparatively higher than those in other cities, which is discouraging.

This book should be interesting not only to Bangaloreans, but also to all urban dwellers, economists, environmentalists, social activists, and policy makers in India and abroad. I wish the book a very good reception from readers, including libraries.

– M V Nadkarni
(Honorary Visiting Professor, Institute for Social &
Economic Change, Bengaluru.)
24 May 2023

Notes

1 See *The Industrial Novels* by Mehmet Akif Balkaya (2015), Cambridge Scholars Publishing, New Castle upon Tyne.

2 This is my translation of a verse in Sanskrit in my *ParisaranītiShatakam – A Century of verses in Sanskrit on Environmental Ethics with translation in English verse and Notes*, in M V Nadkarni (2022): *SāmājikaNītiKāvyaGucchah – A Bouquet of Verses on Social Ethics*, Manipal: Manipal Universal Press.

(Verse 25, pp. 14--15). This book is a collection of five Shatakams (in Sanskrit verse with translation into English verse) including the one from which the verse above is quoted. The other Shatakams are respectively on Gandhian philosophy, Hinduism from a Gandhian perspective, Humanitarianism, and Democracy.

3 Visit http://www.unep.org.

Acknowledgements

Many forces shape what we are, what we do, and how we do things. Gratitude to those forces brings their blessings to achieve further.

Our sincere thanks to renowned expert Prof. M V Nadakarni, who has been a great adviser to this research work. It is also our honour that Professor has taken his precious time in writing an insightful and a thoughtful foreword for this book.

We are also thankful for the invaluable suggestions and advice provided by various experts in the field of Economics like Prof. B S Sreekantaradya, Prof. Bisalaih, Prof. B K Tulasimala, Prof. S Madheswaran, Dr. A V Manjunatha, Ms. B P Vani, and Prof. Indrajit Bairagya, which shaped this research into a publishable work. A deepest gratitude is extended to the administrative and academic section at ISEC.

I am grateful to Routledge Publications for considering this work to publish and special thanks to Ms. Shoma Choudhury and Ms. Shloka Chauhan for their immense support in bringing this work into publishable format.

The book is dedicated to family and friends who have been a constant support in our career.

Abbreviations

ADF	Augmented Dickey Fuller Test
AIC	Akaike Information Criteria
AQEG	Air Quality Expert Group, UK
ARDL	Auto-regressive distributed lag
BBMP	Bruhat Bengaluru Mahanagara Palike
BCG	Boston Consultancy Group
BMRCL	Bengaluru Metro Rail Corporation Ltd.
BMR-RMP	Bengaluru Metropolitan Region-Revised Master Plan
BMTC	Bengaluru Mahanagara Transport Corporation
BP	Breusch–Pagan test
BTP	Bangalore Transport Police
BTRE	Bureau of Infrastructure, Transport and Regional Economics
BUD	Bengaluru Urban District
CAC	Command and Control Measures
CBD	Central Business District
CC	Catalytic Converter
CEBR	Central Economic Bureau of Research
CNG	Compressed natural gas
CO	Carbon monoxide
CO_2	Carbon dioxide
COI	Cost of illness
COMEAP	Committee on the Medical Effects of Air Pollutants
CPCB	Central Pollution Control Board
CRRI	Centre for Road Research Institute
CSIR	Council of Scientific and Industrial Research
CUSUM and CUSUMSQ	Cumulative sum and cumulative sum of squares
CVM	Contingent valuation method
DES	Directorate of Economics and Statistics

DfT	Department of Transport, UK
DULT	Directorate of Urban Land Transport
DW	Durbin–Watson
ECM	Error correction mechanism
ECMT	European Conference of Ministers of Transport
EI	Economic instruments
EPA	Environment Protection Agency
ERP	Electronic road pricing
FWC	Fuel wastage cost
GDP	Gross domestic product
HEI	Health Effect Institute
HOV	High-occupancy vehicles
IBM	International Business Machines Corporations
ICCT	International Council on Clean Transportation
IHME	Institute for Health Metrics and Evaluation
IIHS	Indian Institute for Human Settlements
IIM	Indian Institute of Management
IRC	Indian Road Congress
IT	Information technology
ITS	Intelligent Transport System
JLL	Jones Lang LaSalle
KSPCB	Karnataka State Pollution Control Board
LE):	Egyptian pound
LM	Lagrange multiplier
LOS	Level of service
LPG	Liquefied petroleum gas
LRT	Light rail transport
MFT	Ministry of Transport, New Zealand
MNC	Multinational company
MoRTH	Ministry of Road Transport and Highway
MPC	Marginal private cost
MSC	Marginal social cost
NH	National highway
NHSRC	National Health Systems Resource Centre
NO	Nitric oxide
NOx	Nitrogen oxide
NRCC	National Research Council Committee
NTDPC	National Transport Development Policy Committee
NYC	New York Corporation
OECD	Organisation for Economic Co-operation and Development
ORR	Outer Ring Road
PCI	Per capita income

PHL	Productive hour loss
PM	Particulate matter
PP	Philip Perron test
RBI	Reserve Bank of India
RC	Resource cost
RRR	Relative risk ratio
Rs.	Rupees
RSPM	Respiratory suspended particulate matter
RTO	Regional Transport Office
SIC	Schwartz Information Criteria
SO_2	Sulphur dioxide
SPM	Suspended particulate matter
TCI	Transport Corporation of India
TDC	Time delay cost
TDEC	Total direct economic cost
TDM	Transport demand management
TEC	Total economic cost
TERI	The Energy and Resource Institute
TfL	Transport for London
TIEC	Total indirect economic cost
TMSC	Total marginal social cost
TND	Tunisian Dinar
TOD	Transit-oriented development
TSM	Transport System Management
TTI	Texas Transportation Institute
UITP	International Association of Public Transport
UK	United Kingdom
UN	United Nations
UNCED	United Nations Conference on Environment and Development
USA	United States of America
V/C	Volume-to-capacity ratio
VKT	Vehicle kilometre travelled
VMT	Vehicle metre travelled
VOSL	Value of statistical life
VOTT	Value of traffic time
VTPI	Victoria Transport Policy Institute
WDL	Work-day loss
WHO	World Health Organisation
WPI	Wholesale price index
WTA	Willingness to accept
WTP	Willingness to pay

Chapter 1

Traffic Congestion as an Urban Economic Problem

1.1 Introduction

Transportation is the lifeline of the urban economy. Road transport, especially, acts as a vein in vitalizing economic growth. Unfortunately, the uncontrolled growth of cities has severe side effects. One major effect of rapid urban economic growth is traffic congestion. In developing countries, unprecedented growth in travel demand (more so in private transport) and meagre growth in road transport networks have been inflicting urban economies with major negative externalities like time loss, air pollution, and health impacts. These externalities impose significant costs on the economy. If these costs are accounted for, then internalization, i.e., policy decisions, would be more sustainable. Currently, the traffic congestion problems are handled from the supply side. That means adding more roads to handle traffic flow. But what is required is a paradigm shift towards demand-side management. This shift requires quantification of both economic and environmental costs of traffic congestion, termed as external costs.

Understanding and quantifying such costs is a herculean task due to the complexities involved in its impact. Numerous research studies have proved the existence of a cohesive relationship between the transport sector and economic prosperity (ECMT, 2001; Eddington, 2006; MfT, 2016). A better transport system will reduce travel costs and time. This will have a significant positive impact on the behavioural and economic decisions of society in the form of increased economic opportunities.

However, the benefits of the transport sector are emerging counterproductive to the economy in recent years (Hartgen & Field, 2009; MfT, 2016). Being the product of agglomeration economies coupled with economic growth (Graham & Gibbons, 2019), an upsurge in travel demand in cities is often met by personal vehicular ownership (Dargay et al., 2007; Wu et al., 2014). The existence of poor urban road infrastructure cannot accommodate the unprecedented growth of private vehicles and has caused significant problems with gridlocks and traffic congestion (Goodwin, 2004).

DOI: 10.4324/9781032662299-1

Such obstruction in travel has resulted in a reduction of previously accrued benefits (of reduced travel time and cost).

1.2 Scope and Significance of the Book

Traffic congestion is not a mere planning blunder. It is also connected with behavioural aspects of commuters. But this externality has significant economic implications. The inordinate delays have reduced the opportunity cost of time and increased the resource (fuel) cost, thereby negatively affecting the productivity of the economy (Somuyiwa et al., 2015; Hartgen & Field, 2009). Even the public health and environment (inter-sectoral) are at risk due to the constant exposure to vehicular emissions caused by traffic congestion. If these effects are not accounted for, then internalization becomes difficult.

The novelty of the book lies in the identification and quantification of both economic and environmental externalities of traffic congestion. The book makes an important contribution by identifying the opportunity costs of time stuck in traffic congestion (time delay) as a productivity loss. This cost is proved to have a significant impact on the economy. Many studies have established that traffic congestion has increased pollutants' concentration. But, there is a lack of studies that has quantified its impact. Hence, the book makes a significant contribution to the literature by establishing the causal relationship between the traffic pollutant and health impacts and also quantifying the impacts.

In this book, we have quantified the costs of traffic congestion by taking one of the major metropolitan cities of India. The rationale for selecting an Indian city is these cities are emerging economic powerhouses of the country (elaborated in Chapter 2). This has led to tremendous economic growth getting concentrated in cities with unprecedented growth in private vehicles. This is making urban roads get jammed causing severe delays. Unfortunately, the urban planners have ignored the economic impacts of traffic congestion. They believed that traffic congestion is a mere result of inefficient use of infrastructure, and hence, preferred investment in increasing the road capacities. This instead of solving the problem has further intensified the congestion.

Another delusion of urban planners in developing countries is to follow the policy options adopted by developed economies. This may yield undesirable effects, as the nature of mobility in cities of developing countries is far more different from that of developed countries. For example, the cities of developed countries have homogeneous travel patterns, whereas, in the case of developing countries, traffic mobility is highly heterogeneous (Kiran & Verma, 2016). This heterogeneity lies in different modes of transport operating in the road network simultaneously. Further, the cities of developing countries are growing both geographically and economically posing serious challenges in managing the traffic flow.

In a nutshell, the problem of traffic congestion in developing countries is quite distinctive. It is not only a result of improper urban and infrastructure planning but mainly due to the complex behavioural traits of commuting. In this backdrop, the book explains the nature and implications of traffic congestion (in Chapter 2). The impact of traffic gridlocks is explained by estimating its cost on the economy. The traffic congestion costs are classified as direct and indirect costs (in Chapters 4 and 5). For this, we have taken an important city of Global South, Bengaluru, as a case study (Chapter 3). Understanding the problem and applying the economic principles to this city, the book has also provided evidence on the feasibility of economic instruments in internalizing the traffic congestion effects (in Chapter 6).

1.3 Concept and Approach of Traffic Congestion

The quantification of traffic congestion requires a proper conceptualization of the problem. Although the term 'traffic congestion' is common and widely used, it lacks uniformity in its definition. This is due to varied perceptions of the problem from the user of the road to engineers and economists, which can be grouped into three categories: Users' perspective; Engineers' perspective, and Economist perspective:

i. Users recognize congestion on the road when their travel speed falls below their acceptable level. This is termed as perceived congestion by Wallis and Lupton (2013).
ii. Engineers define traffic congestion as the number of vehicles using the road exceeds the road capacity. This is usually measured using the Level of Service (LOS) indicator with volume/capacity (v/c) ratio (a qualitative measurement to describe the operating condition of a road based on speed, travel time, delay, and safety) (Wallis & Lupton, 2013).
iii. Economists perceive traffic congestion as a classic case of externality. They define the external cost of traffic congestion as the additional cost imposed by an additional road user when the vehicles enter beyond the road capacity.

Such diverse perceptions in definitions complicate further to determine a universally accepted definition. As the road is a public good that characterizes non-excludability and non-rivalry (Dupuit, 1844), it makes the problem of traffic congestion much more complex to define. Since the principal objective of the book is to quantify the costs of traffic congestion imposed on road users and the economy, we adopted a quantifiable definition. Brownfield et al. (2003) defines, 'an urban link (with signalized exit) is defined as congested when traffic cannot exit the urban link within one signal cycle'. This definition was also adopted by DfT (2001) and Lindsey (2007), who considered a stop-and-go pattern as the criteria for urban congestion.

The book adopted the engineering definition for understanding the technicalities of traffic congestion, and for quantifying the external costs of traffic congestion, the economic principles are adopted. Hence, the term traffic congestion is defined as a 'situation where the road users cannot exit the urban link within one signal cycle in the city'.

The definition incorporates approaches namely, engineering and economic approach. These approaches differ in their frameworks. One should remember that traffic congestion is still considered as a subject matter of civil engineering. The engineering framework believed that traffic congestion occurs mainly due to obstruction or inefficient use of roads (Thomson, 1998). This instantly points to the lack of road capacity. The approach revolves around enhancing the physical capacity of the road and the number of vehicles that it can accommodate. Even though the engineering approach measures the costs of traffic congestion, it is limited only to the physical characteristics of the road. The approach defines traffic congestion in terms of the relationship between traffic density and speed. The traffic flow q (vehicle per lane per hour) is the product of traffic density k (vehicle per lane per kilometre) and speed v (km/hour).

$$q = kv \tag{1.1}$$

Eq. (1.1) indicates, other things being equal, as more vehicles enter the road, traffic density increases, travel speed falls, and travel time increases. This traffic flow principle has been a fundamental foundation for the engineering approach. The approach is used to measure costs for evaluating the highway performance, network delay cost, and so on.

The major caveat of this approach lies in estimating the costs by comparing the congested network to free-flow speed. Prud'homme (1998) describes that free-flow comparison wants the road to be empty, which is a naïve approach as empty roads are economically undesirable. Bureau of Infrastructure, Transport and Regional Economics (BTRE) (2015) remarks that having free-flow speed as an ideal speed is economically not justifiable. Many researchers and studies like Wallis and Lupton (2013), Grant-Mullar and Laird (2006), and Transport Canada (2006) supported the same and advocated that such estimates are environmentally unjustifiable.

While the economic approach to traffic congestion differs from the engineering approach in its fundamental understanding of the issue. As against the speed-flow technique, economists recognized the need to determine an optimal traffic flow, an optimal speed and an optimum level of traffic congestion (Thomson, 1998). The approach defines the traffic flow as a sequence of vehicles traversing on a road stretch in the same direction (Arnott, 2015). It advocates the requirement of the desired sequence for the movement of vehicles which will ensure smooth traverse. Vehicle's use beyond this optimal traffic flow is considered to impose additional costs on other vehicle users called external costs of traffic congestion (Wallis & Lupton, 2013).

Instead of considering the free-flow speed of engineering approach, economists considered the optimum speed as efficient. At an optimum speed, vehicles should be able to traverse the road stretch without much delay. If there is a fall in the average speed below the optimum speed, the situation would bc termed as traffic congestion. This speed derives maximum benefit to the road user by achieving the optimal travel of congestion.

Further, the economic approach defines traffic congestion as the additional costs imposed on other road users if the traffic is operating beyond the optimum level. The determination of the optimum level of congestion is termed as 'economic theory of traffic congestion'. This optimal congestion approach calls for a balance between the travel demand and supply of road space (ECMT, 2007).

As we have set the concept and approach to the problem, the book will proceed to provide the framework and impacts of traffic congestion.

1.4 Framework of Traffic Congestion

The growth of a city determines the origin and level of traffic congestion. There are many urban growth models from Alonso (1964) to Krugman (1991) who explored the patterns of city expansion. A key model by Krugman (1991) in his seminal work *Increasing Returns and Economic Geography* provided the inverted U-shaped relationship between transport cost and economic concentration. He elaborates that, as the economic concentration of industries increases, the external cost of travel would also increase. His theoretical framework on decreasing returns due to transport costs explains the influence of traffic congestion on the economic productivity of cities.

The factors contributing to traffic congestion can be explained as an example of the self-reinforcement process with short- and long-term feedback loops. Figure 1.1 provides a framework, which is stimulated by increased economic activity. Commuters behave rationally while making their travel decision, which is mainly influenced by economic principles like the minimization of travel costs and time. The vehicular use (distance travelled), being the engine of the process, is mainly influenced by increasing income levels.

The travel demand is the derived demand for economic activity. Apart from leisure travel, the majority of the trip taken by an individual is related to his/her occupation. This travel demand is often determined by the efficiency of the transport network in the area. Hence, there is a direct interdependency between the economic growth and transport sector. For instance, economic activities get concentrated in a place where there are better transport modes. The transportation system also develops where there are high economic activities. This interlinkage reinforces both increased income and employment opportunities.

The prominent impact of the rising income is found on the modal choice. Using regression analysis, research studies have proved that an increase in

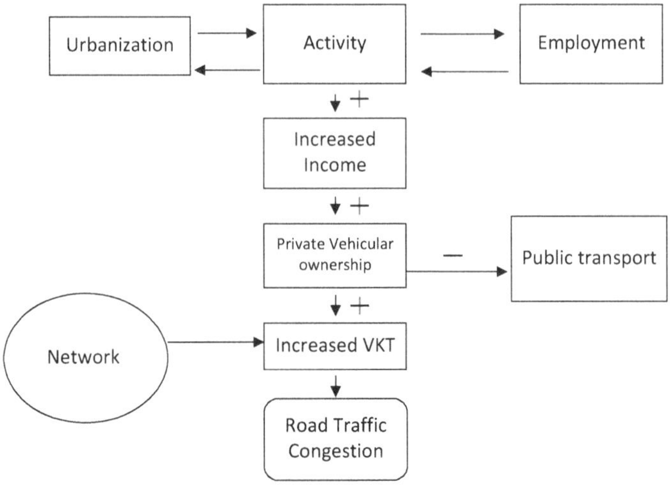

Figure 1.1 Framework of Road Traffic Congestion.
Source: Modified and Adopted from ECMT (2007).

income positively increases car ownership (Ewing et al., 2014; Dargay et al., 2007). Even such relationship is proved in this book for India. Concerning factor is, this has negatively impacted the use of public transportation and non-motorized transport, which act as the feedback loop in the system. Further, as increased private vehicular ownership (vehicle kilometre travelled (VKT)) is not being supported by the existing road network expansion, which intensifies the problem of traffic congestion.

This framework has explained the main reason of traffic congestion. In this background, the book will highlight the key impacts of traffic congestion in the proceeding section.

1.5 Impacts of Traffic Congestion

From the increased travel time to the environmental impacts, traffic congestion as an urban menace has been degrading the quality of life (Bull, 2004). The book classified the impacts of traffic congestion into economic and environmental impacts.

1.5.1 Economic Impacts of Traffic Congestion

One of the major impacts of traffic congestion is the time loss. Several studies on traffic congestion have proved that time loss imposed by queued vehicles has significant economic implications on the commuter and the economy. In the United States, the time cost is estimated at approximately $48 billion per driver in the United States (Arnott & Small, 1994). However, this cost has not accounted for the productivity implication of traffic congestion. If these costs are added, then the above stated cost would go up significantly.

Another consequence of traffic congestion is related to additional fuel expenses. It is a well-known fact that, fuel efficiency peaks at an optimum speed of a vehicle. When the actual speed falls below the optimum speed, the fuel efficiency will reduce (or combustion will increase) (Guttikunda, 2009). For instance, the annual cost of wasted fuel due to congestion in Canada ranged from $176 million to $213 million (50% and 70% thresholds) (Transport Canada, 2006). This estimate provides a glimpse on the resource impact of traffic congestion. However, such studies are lacking in the case of Indian cities.

1.5.2 Environmental Impacts of Traffic Congestion

Generally, environmental impacts are intangible effects of traffic congestion, which are difficult to quantify. Hence, they are often ignored or overlooked during policy decisions. It is estimated that nearly 3 per cent of India's GDP is lost due to air pollution in the country (WHO, 2011). One of the major contributors to this pollution is attributed to vehicular emissions (World Bank, 2015). Vehicular pollutants like carbon monoxide (CO), hydrocarbon (HC), nitrogen oxide (NO_x), Respiratory Suspended Particulate Matter (RSPM), and road dust cause several health-related issues like stress, asthma, cough, and respiratory problems (WHO, 2005). A significant impact of traffic congestion is observed from the highly concentrated vehicular emissions at traffic junctions. Another problem of traffic congestion is noise pollution. Congested traffic creates noise nuisance, impacting both the health and environment of the society.

Developed countries in the world have identified these consequences and initiated several measures to internalize traffic externalities. Issue of concerns lies in developing countries like India, where economic growth takes priority in policy decisions over environmental concerns. In this line, the book considers the externality aspect of the traffic congestion to account for its impacts.

1.6 Conclusion

Although traffic congestion has been a daily urban menace, it has been understood only from the supply side. Slow movement of vehicles tends to have significant economic costs. From the loss of opportunity of time to fuel loss, traffic congestion has huge impact on health of commuters. If these costs are not accounted for, then the policy decision will be lop-sided. Hence, this chapter has provided a framework for understanding the problem from an economic perspective. An economic analysis of traffic congestion requires a sophisticated understanding of the behavioural interactions.

This explains when and where traffic congestion occurs, which should be accompanied by the quantification of economic costs of traffic congestion. The quantification would provide a fundamental understanding of how the effects of traffic congestion can be incorporated in policies. Such policies would improve productivity and quality of life by meeting the mobility needs of society.

References

Arnott, R. (2015). A Bathtub Model of downtown traffic congestion. *Journal of Urban Economics*, *76*, 110–121.

Arnott, R., & Small, K. A. (1994). Economics of traffic congestion. *American Scientist*, *82*(5), 446–455.

Brownfield, J., Graham, A., Eveleigh, H., Ward, H., Robertson, S., & Allsop, R. (2003). Congestion and accident risk. Road Safety Research Report no. 44. DfT.

Bull, A. (Ed.). (2004). *Traffic congestion: The problem and how to deal with it*. United Nations Publications.

Bureau of Infrastructure, Transport and Regional Economics (BTRE). (2015). Traffic and congestion cost trends for Australian capital cities. Department of Infrastructure and regional Development. www.bitre.gov.au

Dargay, J., Gately, D., & Sommer, S. (2007). Vehicle ownership and Income growth worldwide: 1960–2030. *The Energy Journal by International Association for Energy Economics*, *28*(4), 143–170.

Department for Transport. (2001). Perceptions of congestion: Report on qualitative research findings. http://www.dft.gov.uk

Dupuit, J. (1844). *On the measurement of the utility of public works* (D. Murphy, Ed.). Transport, 1968. Penguin.

ECMT (European Conference of Ministers of Transport). (2001). *Assessing the benefits of Transport*. OECD Publication Services. www.oecd.org/cem

ECMT (European Conference of Ministers of Transport). (2007). *Managing urban traffic congestion*. Transport Research Centre. OECD Publication Services. www .oecd-ilibrary.org

Eddington, R. (2006). The Eddington transport study main report: Transport's role in sustaining the UK's productivity and competitiveness. http://www.thepep.org/ClearingHouse/docfiles/Eddington.Transport.Study%20-%20Rod.pdf

Ewing, R., Hamidi, S., Gallican, F., Nelson, A. C., & Grace, J. M. (2014). Structural equation models of VMT growth in US urbanised areas. *Urban Studies*, *51*(14), 3079–3096. https://doi.org/10.1177/0042098013516521

Goodwin, P. B. (2004). The economic costs of road traffic congestion. Discussion paper. Rail Freight Group, Transport Studies Unit, University College London.

Graham, J. D., & Gibbon, S. (2019). Quantifying the wider economic impacts of agglomeration for transport appraisal: Existing evidence and future directions. *Economics of Transportation*, *19*. https://doi.org/10.1016/j.retrec.2019.100121

Grant-Muller, S., & Laird, J. (2006). *Costs of congestion: Literature review of methodology and analytical approaches*. Scottish Executive Social Research.

Guttikunda, S. (2009). Indicative impacts of vehicular idling on air emissions. SIM-air Working Paper series: 18. www.sim-air.org

Hartgen, T. D., & Fields, G. M. (2009). Gridlock and growth: The effect of traffic congestion on regional economic performance. Policy study. Reason foundation. https://reason.org/wp-content/uploads/files/ps371_growth_gridlock_cities_full_study.pdf

Kiran, S., & Verma, A. (2016). Review of studies on mixed traffic flow: Perspectives of developing economies. *Transportation in Developing Economies*, 2(1). https://doi.org/10.1007/s40890-016-0010-0

Krugman, P. (1991). Increasing returns and economic geography. *Journal of Political Economy*, 99(3), 484–499.

Lindsey, C. R. (2007). Congestion relief: Assessing the case for road tolls in Canada. C.D. Howe Institute Commentary. C.D. Howe Institute. Issue. 248.

MfT (Ministry of Transport, New Zealand). (2016). Contribution of transport to economic development: Economic development and transport project summary report. https://www.transport.govt.nz/assets/uploads/our-work/documents/03f6cc62af/edt-contribution-of-transport-to-economic-development.pdf

Prud'homme, R. (1998). Road congestion cost in the Paris area. Paper presented for the 8th World Conference on Transportation Research.

Somuyiwa, A. O., Fadare, S. O., & Ayantoyinbo, B. B. (2015). Analysis of the cost of Traffic congestion on worker's productivity in a mega city of a developing economy. *International Review of Management and Business Research*, 4(3), 654–656.

Thomson, I. J. M. (1998). Reflections on the economics of traffic congestion. *Journal of Transport Economics and Policy*, 32, 93–112.

TomTom (2020). TomTom Congestion Index, TomTom International, Retrieved from HYPERLINK "http://www.tomtom.com"www.tomtom.com.

Transport Canada. (2006). The cost of urban congestion in Canada. Transport Department.

Wallis, I., & Lupton, D. (2013). The costs of congestion reappraised. NZ Transport Agency research report. 489. 65.

WHO (World Health Organization). (2005). *Health effects of transport-related air pollution* (M. Krzyanowski, B. Kuna-Dibbert & J. Schneider, Eds.). WHO Regional Office for Europe.

WHO (World Health Organization). (2011). Top 100 cities with the worst air quality in the world. Urban Emissions. Info. http://urbanemissions.blogspot.com/2013

World Bank. (2015). The global health cost of ambient PM2.5 air pollution. PMEH, World Bank.

Wu, T., Zhao, H., & Ou, X. (2014). Vehicle ownership analysis based on GDP per capita in China: 1963–2050. *Sustainability*, 6, 4877–4899.

Chapter 2

Growth of Road Transport in India

2.1 Introduction

We know that the problem of traffic congestion is an urban menace. But the developed countries are somehow able to manage their traffic problems. This is mainly due to fully developed infrastructure and availability of scientific methods and data sets. But such is not a situation in developing countries. We have already stated in the previous chapter that developing countries are struggling to manage both supply and demand side of travel. Particularly in India, the rapid economic growth is highly concentrated in the metropolitan cities. We can assure that the Indian cities are economic powerhouses. This economic growth has brought tremendous stress on the transport infrastructure. The economic concentration in cities made urban mobility a serious concern. In this chapter, we will explore the growth of road transport in India and also in major metropolitan cities. The relationship between economic growth and its impact on the road transport (vehicular growth) is scientifically examined using econometric tools. It is evident that, such a growth is observed in many metropolitan cities of other developing countries.

2.2 India's Economic Development and Growth of Road Transport Sector

The growth linkage between India's GDP and its transport sector is growing strong in recent decades. For instance, the contribution of the transport sector to the total GDP stood at 4.8 per cent. In this, the major contribution was by road transport of about 3.1 per cent, whereas the railways contribute merely 0.9 per cent and remaining 0.8 per cent by other modes of transportation in 2017–2018 (TERI, 2018–2019). This signifies that the road transport sector is one of the fastest-growing sectors in the economy. Further, among different modes, rail and road share a dominant traffic performance of 87 per cent. Among them, road transport alone has a modal traffic performance of 62 per cent (NTDPC, 2014). This indicates the economic importance of road transport. TCI and IIM study (2012) highlighted that India's freight volume

DOI: 10.4324/9781032662299-2

is increasing at a compound annual growth rate (CAGR) of 9.08 per cent and passenger vehicles at 10.76 per cent. However, the road length is increasing at 4.01 per cent in 2011. This point at a lead-lag relationship between the growing personalized vehicular ownership and road length. Hence, causing severe negative externalities like traffic congestion and air pollution.

Theories related to urbanization (Alonso, 1964), spatial interaction models (Krugman, 1991), and industrial location (Marshall, 1891) have advocated that concentration of economic activity in a location brings economies of scale. Such economies of scale attract more industries, making the place more attractive (urbanization) to employment. This employment leads to an increased income level of the location, which again causes the growth of vehicular population. Bayliss (1981) opines that growth in vehicular ownership is continuing hand in hand with rapid urbanization. Button (1993) states that, such an increase in vehicular ownership, primarily due to urbanization coupled with employment opportunities has put high pressure on road traffic. Numerous studies have proved this relationship empirically (Dargay et al., 2007; Eakins, 2013; Ewing et al., 2014). Strong evidence is found on the relationship between income and fuel cost of driving with the level of urbanization and vehicular kilometre travelled (Grimal et al., 2013; Bastian et al., 2016; Stapleton et al., 2017; Dft, 2018). To examine such relationship in case of India, Figure 2.1 plots income and vehicular growth. The income is represented in terms of per capita income (PCI) at constant prices of 2011–2012 and vehicular growth is taken as number of vehicles per 1,000 persons.

From Figure 2.1, it gives a strong intuition that the income and vehicular ownership are correlated. The per capita income which was Rs. 12,757 in

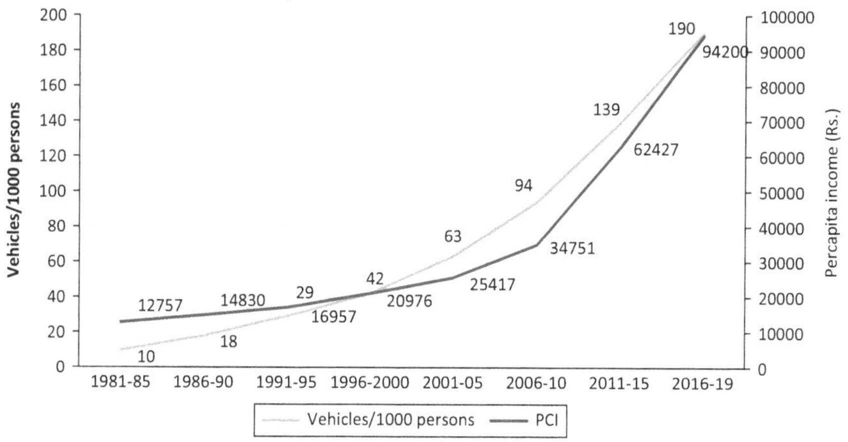

Figure 2.1 Vehicles[a] Per 1,000 Persons and Per Capita Income[b] in India.

Source: Authors' Analysis Based on MORTH & RBI data. [a]Total Registered Vehicles (Including Private, Public, and Goods Vehicles); [b]PCI at Constant Prices of 2011–2012.

1981–1985 increased around seven times to Rs. 94,200 in 2016–2019 showing around 6.3 per cent of annual growth. However, vehicle per thousand population which was just 10 per 1,000 persons in 1981–1985 has increased more than 18 times to 190 by 2016–2019 showing approximately 17.6 per cent growth. This rapid increase in vehicular population has become a matter of grave concern due to severe traffic gridlocks in many cities of the country.

Further, the relationship between the urbanization and working-age population growth is captured in Figure 2.2. It is interesting to note that the total vehicular population in million-plus cities accounted for about 30 per cent of the total vehicular population of the country. The per capita vehicles to urban population which was 36 vehicles per 1,000 persons in 1981–1985 has increased to 495 vehicles per 1,000 persons in 2016–2019, which is showing a 12.75 per cent growth rate. Similarly, vehicles per 1,000 working-age persons were just 15 in 1981–1985, which has increased to 274 vehicles in 2018–2019.

Though we examine those variables like income, urbanization and working population have a positive link with the vehicular population, and this needs to be tested empirically. The basic economic theories have proved that economic growth and urbanization are positively linked. Marshall (1890) stated that there is a strong influence of urbanization by increasing the employment opportunities and income, which tend to have a positive impact on consumer's expenditure on comfort goods. One important comfort good is to opt a private mode of travel. Even many studies like Medlock and Soligo (2001) and

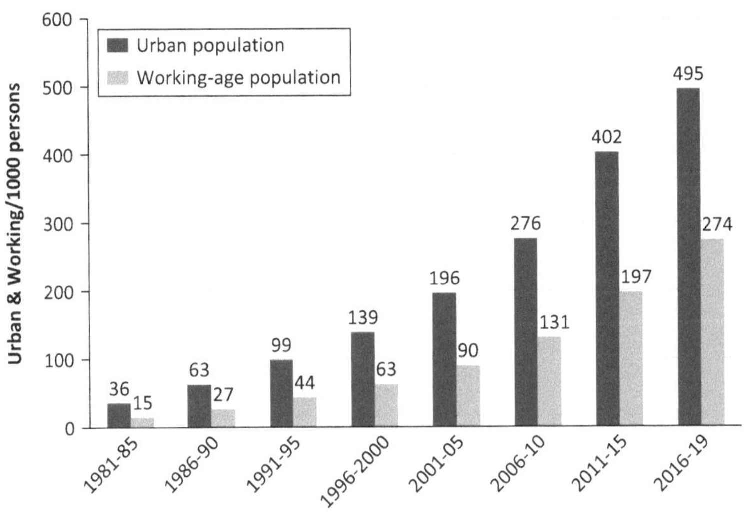

Figure 2.2 Growth of Vehicle Population Per 1,000 Urban and Working Population.

Source: Authors' Analysis Based on MORTH & UN Data.

Eddington (2006) confirmed an existence of a positive relationship between vehicular ownership and income. Owing to these theoretical backgrounds, we established empirical evidence by using time-series econometric analysis.

2.2.1 Time-Series Econometric Analysis of the Relationship: Data and Methodology

Based on the previous theoretical discussion, we have considered the following variables (in Table 2.1) for the analysis. The period of the data is from 1980 to 2019 with the annual series.

The regression equation (2.1) is specified to know the impact of income, urbanization, and fuel prices on the personal vehicular ownership:

$$\ln(pvhcl_t) = \beta_0 + \beta_1 \ln(pci) + \beta_2 \ln(urb) + \beta_3 (wpi\_f) + u_t \quad (2.1)$$

Ln represents the natural log form of the series to linearize the trend. Parameters β_0 is constant, $\beta_1,$ $\beta_2,$ β_3 are long-run elasticities of pci, urb, and wpi_f, respectively, and u_t represents the residual term. A time dummy, namely dummy 1991 is used in the analysis exogenously to control for any structural effect if it exists.[1] The year 1991 is significant in Indian economic history as the major economic reforms were introduced, which has a significant impact on the income and purchasing trends of Indian consumers.

Prior to the cointegration analysis, the variables are tested for any causality. Using Granger causality test, we found that the variables in the model do not have any bi-directional causality. Hence, the model can be preceded with the further analysis. Since, the variables are in time-series order, the data are tested for the stationarity. Using Augumented Dickey–Fuller (ADF) test, we found that, *pvhcl, pci*, and *wpi*_f are stationary at first difference (I(0)) and *urb* variable is stationary at level (I(0)). This means that the variables are of mixed order. Hence, the model is restricted to use the popular methods of cointegration like Engle and Granger (1987) test or Johansen–Juselius (1990) test.

Table 2.1 Description and sources of variables

Variables	*Description*	*Source*
Private vehicles (pvhcl)-dependent variable	Total registered private vehicles (car, two-wheelers, jeeps)	MoRTH 2018
Per capita income (PCI)	GDP per capita at constant prices (2011–2012)	RBI
Urbanization (urb)	Urban population	World urbanization prospects
WPI_fuel (wpi_f)	Wholesale price index of petroleum products (constant prices of 2011–2012)	Ministry of Petroleum and Natural Gas

To overcome the limitations of these tests, Pesaran, Shin, and Smith (2001) and Pesaran and Shin (1999) have developed an alternative approach called Autoregressive Distributed Lag (ARDL). This approach gained popularity over other methods by providing inclusion of variables at a different order. That means the approach can be adopted for models whose variables are in I (1) or I (0) or even fractionally integrated (Pesaran & Pesaran, 1997). A major advantage of ARDL is, it corrects for both residual correlation and endogenity problem among the variables. Hence, the ARDL approach to cointegration provides robust and consistent results of long-run coefficients (Pesaran & Shin, 1999).

$$\begin{aligned}\Delta \ln(pvhcl) &= \beta_0 \sum_{i-1}^{q} \beta_{1i} \Delta \ln(pvhcl_{t-i}) + \sum_{i-1}^{q} \beta_{2i} \Delta \ln(pci_{t-i}) \\ &+ \sum_{i-1}^{q} \beta_{3i} \Delta \ln(urb_{t-i}) + \sum_{i-1}^{q} \beta_{4i} \Delta wpi(f)_{t-i} + \beta_5 \ln(pvhcl_{t-1}) \\ &+ \beta_6 \ln(pci_{t-1}) + \beta_7 \ln(urb_{t-1}) + \beta_8 (wpi\_f)_{t-1} + u_t\end{aligned} \tag{2.2}$$

where Δ is the first difference operator, q is optimal lag length, β_0 is constant, β_1, β_2, β_3, and β_4 represents short-run dynamics and β_5, β_6, β_7, and β_8 are long-run elasticities. ARDL model of co-integrating vector is reparametrized into Error Correction Mechanism (ECM). The error correction model for Equation (4.2) is given in Equation (2.2).

$$\begin{aligned}\Delta \ln(pvhcl) &= \beta_0 \sum_{i-1}^{q1} \beta_{1i} \Delta \ln(pvhcl_{t-i}) + \sum_{i-1}^{q2} \beta_{2i} \Delta \ln(pci_{t-i}) \\ &+ \sum_{i-1}^{q3} \beta_{3i} \Delta \ln(urb_{t-i}) + \sum_{i-1}^{q4} \beta_{4i} \Delta (wpi\_f)_{t-i} + \lambda_1 EC_{t-1} + \varepsilon_t\end{aligned} \tag{2.3}$$

Where q_1, q_2, q_3, and q_4 indicate optimal lag length λ is the speed of adjustment to equilibrium and EC is the error correction term derived from long-run equation. For the cointegration, these coefficients must be significantly different from zero and estimates of them must not be too large (it must lie between 0 and −1). The reparametrized result gives short-run dynamics and the long-run relationship of the variables (Nkaro & Uko, 2016). In order to find out the long-run relationship, Bound F statistics is conducted with two bounds, i.e., lower and upper bound.

H_0 (null hypothesis) – there is no cointegration among variables.

The rule of thumb is, if calculated F-statistic is greater than the upper bound, then the null hypothesis is rejected, and if it is less than lower bound, the null hypothesis is accepted and if it falls between the lower and upper bound, the test is inconclusive. With respect to lag length, the AIC (Akaike Information Criterion) and SIC (Schwarz Information Criterion) give the optimal lag

Table 2.2 Long-run coefficients of ARDL

Regressor	*Coefficient*	*t-ratio*
ln(pci)	0.38[a]	0.04
ln(urb)	0.36[b]	0.25
wpi_f	−0.003[a]	−1.47
Constant	−61.41[b]	−2.81

length as two. Since the data are in the annual series, it is expected that the impact will be captured with a lag of one or two years.

2.2.2 Result and Discussion

The short- and long-run result of the model is given in Table 2.2. From the model, it can be seen that the variables under consideration have a positive impact on private vehicles. To state, 1 per cent increase in per capita income will increase the private vehicular population by 0.38 per cent. Further, 1 per cent increase in urbanization will increase the private vehicular population by 0.36 per cent. The result of the fuel price index signifies that there is an inverse relationship between fuel price and vehicular population. These findings are in line with the results by Ewing et al. (2014), Dargay et al. (2007), and Stapleton et al. (2017).

Short-run estimates[c]

Δlnpvhcl = −0.66	ECM[b] +0.36	lnvhcl(−1)[b] +	4.8lnurb [b]– 0.001	Δwpi_f[a]	−0.27d91
(−4.7)	(−3.2)	(5.4)	(−1.15)	(4.7)	

R^2 = 0.66; Adj R^2 = 0.63; DW: 2.0.
[a]Significant at 5% level; [b]Significant at 1% level; [c]*t*-values are in parenthesis; [d]Significant at 10% level.

The short-run error correction (EC) term in the model is negative and significant. This indicates that there exists a cointegration among the variables. The speed of adjustment is –0.66 indicating around 66 per cent of the disequilibrium is corrected within a year. The model is verified with the F-statistics to know the long-run cointegration. The computed F-statistics (3.89) is lying above the critical upper bound I (1) values (3.2). According to Pesaran and Pesaran (1996) & Pesaran et al. (2001), this confirms that the variables have long-run relationships and thereby rejects the null hypothesis. Further the model is test for serial correlation (LM test) and heteroskedasticity (BP test). Even the stability test (since the data is time-series) like CUSUM and

CUSUMSQ are tested (refer to Appendixes 2.1 and 2.2). The results indicate that the model is structurally stable and reliable.

As we have proved the impact of economic and demographic variable on the vehicular growth at the macro level, we will proceed to examine the road transport sector growth in metropolitan cities of India. As stated earlier, it is in these cities that we encounter the problem of traffic congestion.

2.3 Indian Metropolitan Cities and Road Transport Sector

The world lives in urban areas. World Urbanization Report (2021) estimates show that approximately 55 per cent of the world population resides in cities. As cities are the economic powerhouse, nearly 60 per cent of the world GDP is contributed by them. Indian cities are not an exception. They contribute a whopping 63 per cent to the GDP and is expected to increase about 70 per cent by 2030. These cities are home for around 31 per cent of the total population (Census, 2011), and nearly 182.4 million vehicles are plying on narrow and highly congested roads. The economic growth in cities looks very promising with improvement in the standard of living. This has created more demand for the private mode of transport. Unfortunately, such growth of vehicles is not accompanied by the supporting infrastructures like growth of road length, scientific traffic management system, and improved public transport resulting in crawling traffic and air pollution. To examine this, we have taken five major metropolitan cities of the country based on their population and vehicular growth.

Apart from the two most populous cities, namely, Mumbai and New Delhi, tremendous growth trend is observed in south cities namely, Chennai and Bengaluru. Since the data relates to 2011 census, Bengaluru ranks the fifth largest metropolitan city in the country. But, the recent population estimates by various agencies (UNO, 2017) state that the city has crossed the population of Chennai city and is home for more than 10.41 million people and is predicted to be 15 million by 2030 (UNO, 2017). Even in geographical terms, the city is growing rapidly (Chapter 3). Table 2.3 provides the geographic and demographic details of the cities.

The information regarding the road length indicates that next to New Delhi, Bengaluru ranks second in the position for road length. Though this indicates that Bengaluru has better road network, but when it is compared to vehicular growth, the city suffers from severe form of traffic congestion. Table 2.4 provides the growth of vehicular density in each metropolitan city.

We can observe that there is a leaping growth of vehicular density in all the cities. The matter of concern lies in cities like Bengaluru and Chennai, where the vehicular density is increasing at a higher rate. This highlights the intensity of traffic congestion, especially in a fast-emerging city like Bengaluru. In terms of motorization rate (refer Figure 2.3), Bengaluru ranks second next to

Table 2.3 Geographic and demographic details of metropolitan cities

Metropolitan cities[2]	*Population (2011)*	*Area (sq. kms)*	*Road length (kms)*
Mumbai	18,414,288	603.4	2,000
New Delhi	16,314,838	1,484	28,500
Kolkata[3]	14,112,536	205	4,636
Chennai	8,696,010	426	2,847
Bengaluru	8,499,399	709	10,200

Source: Respective city's corporation websites and Census 2011.

Table 2.4 Vehicular density in metropolitan cities

Metropolitan cities	*Vehicular density (vehicles/sq.kms)*	
	2001	*2011*
Mumbai	1,708	3,101
Delhi	2,446	4,865
Kolkata	3,729	4,054
Bengaluru	2,228	5,345
Chennai	2,957	5,098

Source: Authors' analysis from Census, MoRTH, 2001 & 2011.

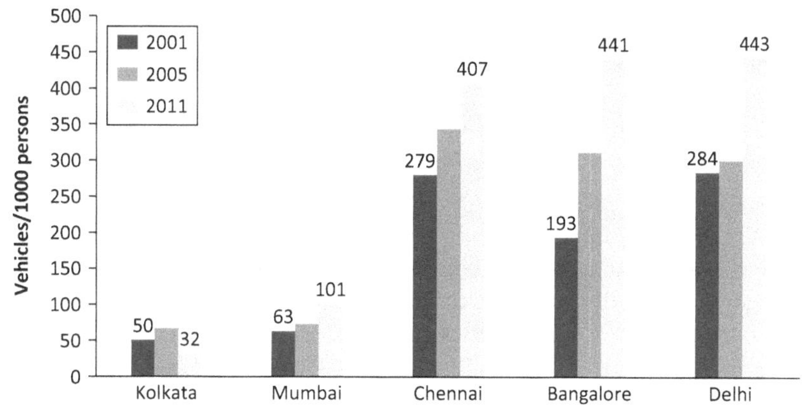

Figure 2.3 Motorization Rate in Metropolitan Cities.

Source: Authors' Analysis Based on MoRTH Data (2001–2011).

Table 2.5 Modal split in metropolitan cities

Cities	*2001*		*2011*	
	Two-wheelers/ 1,000 people	*Cars/1,000 people*	*Two-wheelers/ 1,000 people*	*Cars/1,000 people*
Mumbai	34	20	57	30
Delhi	179	74	269	130
Kolkata	29	24	13	14
Chennai	210	53	267	66
Bengaluru	252	50	308	83
All India	**52**	**07**	**86**	**16**

Source: Authors' Analysis from MoRTH Report and Census 2001&2011.

New Delhi. The motorization rate is the total registered vehicles per 1,000 person in each city.

Additionally, to examine the intensity of the motorization rate, Table 2.5 provides the modal-wise vehicular density in the metropolitan cities for the period 2001 and 2011. The motorization rate of personal vehicles, mainly two-wheelers and cars in all the cities are increasing at an unprecedented rate. But the rise in the density is astounding in Bengaluru city.

The city tops with two-wheeler population (308 two-wheelers/1,000 persons) among all the cities in the country. This growth can be attributed to lack of adequate public transportation services, increasing economic concentration of industries and service sectors, economic migration, changing urban lifestyles. To capture the inadequacy in public transportation, the next section examines the share and growth of public transportation in the metropolitan cities[4].

2.3.1 *Share of Public Transportation in Metropolitan Cities*

Cities of the world have proved that increasing mobility can be met by expanding public transportation. US Environmental Protection Agency (USEPA, 2008) recommended that at least half of the population of the area should use public transport to achieve sustainable mobility. This would help in the conservation of fuel resources and lessen pollution in the environment. Abiding by this, most of the cities of the developed world have improved their public transportation to address the sustainability issues of the transport sector in recent years. For instance, in New York, almost 60 per cent of the reported commuting is undertaken in the public mode of transportation (NYC Mobility Report, 2018), while in London, the share of public transport users is 37 per cent of the total transport users (TfL, 2018). Paris holds a good record with 70 per cent of daily commuters using public transportation (Global Mobility Report, 2017).

Table 2.6 Share of public transport usage in cities

Metropolitan cities	*Share of public transport usage (%)*
Mumbai	13
New Delhi	21
Kolkata	22
Chennai	19
Bengaluru	20

Source: Census, 2011.

On the contrary, the story of Indian cities differs from that of the developed world. The share of public transportation in many cities is worryingly low. The main reasons are lack of investment and inefficiencies in the public transport sector. This has led to preference towards private modes of travel. The share of public transport users in these metropolitan cities (Table 2.6) are compared using Census (2011) data. The data give the percentage share of public transport users to total modal share in each city. It is astounding to observe that, none of the cities in the country have public modal share more than 25 per cent. This indicates poor performance of public transport.

The above analysis has brought out the intensity of the problem in the major metropolitan cities of the country. Another dimension through which the intensity can be analyzed is the impact of vehicular growth on the environment. To validate this, the air quality level in metropolitan cities of the country is analyzed in the next section.

2.4 Traffic Congestion and Air Pollution in Metropolitan Cities

Vehicular emissions are considered to be the major source of air pollution main in metropolitan cities. Further, it is attributed that air pollution is the leading cause of health risk in many cities (World Bank & IHME, 2016). Air pollution is considered as a third fatal risk factor of death in a low and middle-income country, and India is not free among them. In the case of India, it is reported that annually around 6.2 lakh premature deaths occur due to air pollution in cities (Roychowdhury, 2013). The fatal risk of air pollution has cost 8.5 per cent of GDP, which majorly attributed to the pollutants like PM_{10} in 2013 (World Bank & IHME, 2016). Among various air pollutants, particulate matter 2.5 has been considered as the most dangerous pollutant for human health.

World Bank (2013) study reported that the major source of $PM_{2.5}$ is due to vehicular emissions. This has been even substantiated by TERI (2015) for

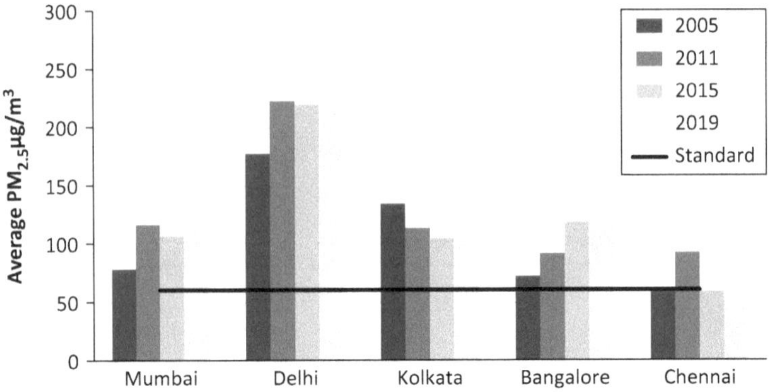

Figure 2.4 Level of Average $PM_{2.5}$ µg/m³ in Metropolitan Cities.

Source: CPCB of Various Years.

India. The major contributor of $PM_{2.5}$ is the transport sector with a dominant share of 45 per cent and industries by 28 per cent and rest by other sources (TERI, 2015). To examine this, the average $PM_{2.5}$ in the metropolitan cities has been portrayed in Figure 2.4. The data clearly shows that the level of $PM_{2.5}$ has crossed above its standard (60 µg/m³) in all the metropolitan cities indicating degraded air quality level, which is mainly attributed to vehicular emissions.

2.5 Conclusion

The chapter has examined the main factors causing traffic congestion at the macro level. Using the time-series analysis, we proved that economic factors like PCI, urbanization, and fuel price index have a significant impact on the growth of private vehicular population. We have also provided evidence of the inefficiencies in the road transport sector in major metropolitan cities of the country. Due to unprecedented growth in private transportation and meagre growth in public transit, the metropolitan cities of the country are stuck in the snarled-up traffic and degraded air quality level. This has been affecting not only the health and environment but also the economy of these cities. Matter of grave concern lies in the emerging city Bengaluru, where the transport externalities have much relentless impact on the economy. As the city is yet to develop its public transport network, but the rate of urbanization and mobility is already speeding up at incredible pace causing severe traffic congestion. The intensity of this has been explored in Chapter 3.

Notes

1 Properly specified dummy does not affect asymptotic null distribution (Luktepohl, 2004).

2 Cities' name represents the metropolitan jurisdiction of the city.
3 The city is selected mainly because of its high population and historical importance in the transport sector.
4 Other factors lack reliable data for all the cities.

References

Alonso, W. (1964). *Location and land use*. Harvard University Press.

Bastian, A., Borjesson, M., & Eliasson, J. (2016). Explaining 'peak car' with economic variables. *Transportation Research. Part A: Policy and Practice*, *88*, 236–250.

Bayliss, D. (1981). One billion new city dweller-How will they travel? *Transportation*, *10*, 314–343.

Button, K. J. (1993). *Transport economics* (2nd ed.). Edward Elgar.

Census of India. (2001 [2011]). Population data. http://censusindia.gov.in/

Census Report of Karnataka. (2001 & 2011). Population data. www.census2011.co.in › Karnataka › District List.

CPCB (Central Pollution Control Board). (2005–2013). Annual reports on air pollution. CPCB. www.cpcbenvis.nic.in

Dargay, J., Gately, D., & Sommer, S. (2007). Vehicle ownership and income growth worldwide: 1960–2030. *The Energy Journal by International Association for Energy Economics*, *28*(4), 143–170.

Dft (Department for Transport). (2018). Latest evidence on factors impacting road traffic growth: An evidence review. Department for Transport. Project No. 1–396. www.wsp.com

Eakins, J. (2013). The determinants of household car ownership: Empirical evident from the Irish household budget survey. *International Journal of Transport Economics*, *XLII*(3), 315–342.

Eddington, R. (2006). The Eddington Transport Study main report: Transport's role in sustaining the UK's productivity and competitiveness. http://www.thepep.org/ClearingHouse/docfiles/Eddington.Transport.Study%20-%20Rod.pdf

Engle, R., & Granger, C. (1987). Cointegration and error correction: Representation, estimation and testing. *Econometrica*, *55*(2), 251–276.

Ewing, R., Hamidi, S., Gallican, F., Nelson, A. C., & Grace, J. M. (2014). Structural equation models of VMT growth in US urbanised areas. *Urban Studies*, *51*(14), 3079–3096. https://doi.org/10.1177/0042098013516521

Global Mobility Report. (2017). https://sustainabledevelopment.un.org/content/documents/2643Global_Mobility_Report_2017.pdf

Grimal, R., Collect, R., & Madre, J. L. (2013). Is the stagnation of individual car travel a general phenomenon in France? A time series analysis by zone of residence and standard of living. *Transport Review*, *33*(3), 291–309.

Johansen, S., & Juselius, K. (1990). Maximum likelihood estimation and inference on cointegration-with application to the demand for money. *Oxford Bulletin of Economics and Statistics*, *52*(2), 169–210.

Krugman, P. (1991). Increasing returns and economic geography. *Journal of Political Economy*, *99*, 484–499.

Lutkepohl, H. (2004). Vector autoregressive and vector error correction models. In H. Lutkepohl & M. Kratzig (Eds.), *Applied time series econometrics*. Cambridge University Press.

Marshall, A. (1890). *Principles of economics*. Macmillan.

Medlock, B. K., & Soligo, R. (2001). Economic development and end-use energy demand. *The Energy Journal*, *22*(2), 77–105.

MoRTH (Ministry of Road Transport and Highways). (2011–18). Basic road transport statistics. MoRTH. www.morth.nic.ac

MoRTH (Ministry of Road Transport and Highways). (2015). *Road transport year book 2012–13*. Transport Research Wing. MoRTH. Government of India. www.morth.nic.ac

Nkoro, E., & Uko, K. A. (2016). Autoregressive Distributed Lag (ARDL) cointegration technique: Application and interpretation. *Journal of Statistical and Econometric Methods*, *5*(4), 63–91.

NTDPC (National Transport Development Policy Committee). (2014). India transport report: Moving India to 2032. NTDPC. www.irtpms.in

NYC Mobility Report. (2018). http://www.nyc.gov/html/dot/downloads/pdf/mobility-report-2018-print.pdf

Pesaran, H. M., & Pesaran, B. (1997). *Microfit 4.0: Interactive econometric analysis*. Oxford University Press.

Pesaran, H. M., & Shin, Y. (1991). An autoregressive distributed lag modelling approach to cointegration analysis. In S. Strom, A. Holly, & P. Diamond (Eds.), *Centennial Volume of Ragnar Frisch*. Cambridge University Press.

Pesaran, H. M., Shin, Y., & Smith, I. R. (2001). Bound testing approaches the analysis of level relationship. *Journal of Applied Econometrics*, *16*, 289–326.

Roychowdhury, A. (2013). Good news and bad news: Clearing the air in Indian cities. Centre for Science and Environment.

Stapleton, L., Sorrell, S., & Schwanen, T. (2017). Peak car and increasing rebound: A closer look at car travel trends in Great Britain. *Transportation Research: Part D: Transport and Environment*, *53*, 217–233.

The Energy and Resource Institute (TERI). (2015). Air pollution and health. Discussion Paper by the Energy and Resource Institute: New Delhi. TERI.

The Energy and Resource Institute (TERI). (2019). *TERI energy and environment data diary and yearbook 2017/18*. TERI.

TfL (Transport for London). (2018). Travel in London: II. TfL.

Transport Corporation of India & Indian Institute of Management. (2012). Operational efficient of national highways and freight transport in India (2011–12). A Joint Study report by TCI and IIM Calcutta (3rd ed.). TCI.

UN (United Nations). (2017). World cities 2016. Economic and Social Affairs, UN.

USEPA (United States Environmental Protection Agency). (2008). Sustainability and U.S. EPA. USEPA. https://archive.epa.gov/region9/science/web/pdf/green-book.pdf

World Bank and Institute for Health Metrics and Evaluation (IHME). (2016). The cost of air pollution: Strengthening the economic case for action. World Bank.

World Urbanisation Report. (2015). Cities for all. World Bank.

World Bank. (2013). Diagnostic assessment of select environmental challenges in India: An assessment of physical and monetary losses of environmental health and natural resources. Vol I. World Bank.

Chapter 3

The Problem of Traffic Congestion in Bengaluru

3.1 Introduction

Bengaluru, an attractive hub of Information Technology (IT) sector of the country, has its unique place in India's metropolitan city status. Being the fifth largest metropolitan city in the country (with 8.4 million population) (Census, 2011), it has been declared as 'the most dynamic city of the world', recently (JLL, 2020). Recognized as the Silicon Valley of India, Bengaluru has grown both in terms of population and geographical area. The paradoxical situation of the city is that despite being the most dynamic metropolitan city in the world, the city has been identified for its worst form of traffic congestion in the world (IBM, 2011; TomTom index, 2020).

The city is known for being the Pensioners' Paradise and has started attracting major MNCs after liberalization. This eventually attracted migrants and led to a urban sprawl. Unfortunately, the growth is not being absorbed by the commensurate growth in road infrastructure causing severe forms of traffic gridlocks in the city, and hence imposing both economic and environmental externalities on urban commuters. Though the city has a significant economic importance, there is a severe dearth of comprehensive studies which account for the external costs of traffic congestion. Hence, leaving a huge gap in the transport economics literature. Even studies which attempted to quantify the costs of traffic congestion for other cities have adopted an engineering approach leading to lop-sided transport policy measures. In this respect, the book makes a significant contribution by accounting for both direct (economic) and indirect (environmental) costs of traffic congestion for Bengaluru city. Similar techniques can be adopted to other metropolitan cities to arrive at sustainable transport policies.

In this backdrop, the current chapter begins by examining the nature and causes of traffic congestion in Bengaluru and also the status of its road transport sector. Later, we proceed to provide the details on sample data collected, as there is a dearth of secondary information on travel pattern of commuters. The details of primary data are explored, which sets a background for the estimation process.

DOI: 10.4324/9781032662299-3

3.2 Profile of the City: Demographic Details

The population growth rate in the city has been an interesting impetus for the present study. Being the capital city of Karnataka state, Bengaluru's population is increasing at a much faster rate than the State's population growth (31.54 per cent in 2001–2011). The city's population, which was 63.27 lakhs in 2001, increased to 96.2 lakhs in 2011 showing a 48.3 per cent increase (which was 37.7 per cent in 1991–2001). The city (BBMP) homes 15.69 per cent of the State's population (2011) and 87.75 per cent of the district population and contributes 34 per cent of state's GDP. The population in the city is growing at an annual growth rate of 3.67 per cent from 2001 to 2011. This is much higher than the national growth rate (1.64 per cent). If the population of the city continues to grow at this rate, it is expected to cross more than two crores in 2031 (forecasted from Census data).

Further, like every other city of the world, Bengaluru is also home to a large section of the migrant population. Total migrants in the city have increased from 28.65 per cent in 1991 to 46.8 per cent in 2011 (District Census, 2011) which might increase beyond 50 per cent in the coming year as the city has been attracting population for employment, education, and livelihood opportunities.

There is a tremendous growth in the city's population from just four lakh persons in 1941 to almost over 96.2 lakhs by 2011. To accommodate this huge growth in population, the geographical area has also started increasing from 93 sq. kms in 1941 to over 709.4 sq. kms by 2011 (Census data). This identifies that the city is growing at an alarming rate with severe overcrowding and traffic congestion problems.

3.2.1 Economic Growth and Traffic Congestion in the City

Being one of the 'next decade's fastest-growing city' of the world (Forbes, 2017), the city's per capita income (Rs. 4,96,208 in 2018–2019[1]) ranks above nations' average per capita income (PCI) (Rs. 1,05,526 at constant prices of 2011–2012). With 14 per cent growth rate in the PCI, the city stands as the fourth-highest among major metropolitan cities of the country. This growth in income has a positive impact on total vehicular ownership, which is growing at 11 per cent annually (2001–2019). By this, the city is now the home of the second-highest vehicular population (next to New Delhi) among the metropolitan cities of India. To provide further insights about the city's growing traffic intensity, Figure 3.1 plots the vehicular population and per capita income (at constant prices of 2011–2012) growth of the city. The figure clearly shows that the vehicular population which was 15.96 lakh in 2001 got a five-fold increase in 2019 by almost 85.6 lakh vehicles (Transport Karnataka[2], 2018).

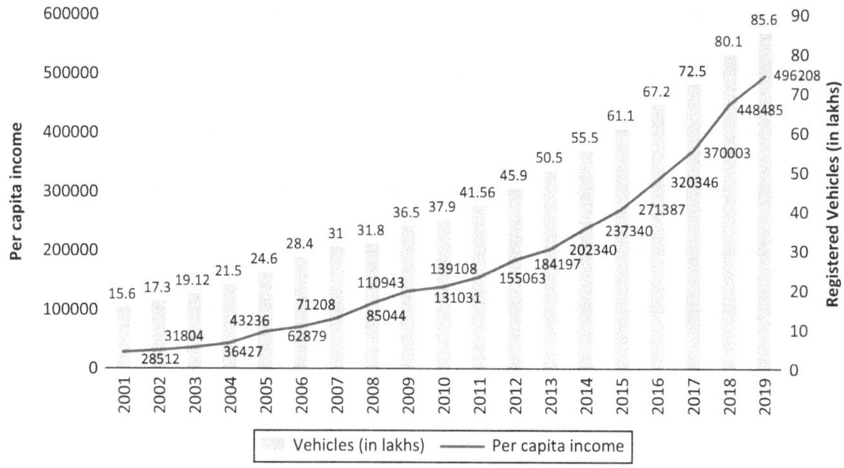

Figure 3.1 Income and Total Vehicular Population in Bengaluru City.

Source: Estimation based on Karnataka Transport Department data 2017–2018.

We know that the main culprit of traffic gridlocks is the growth in private vehicles. To provide evidence for this, Figure 3.2 plots the share of private and public transport vehicles to the total vehicles in the city.

Over the years (from 1971 to 2019), the share of private vehicles to the total vehicles has increased at an exceptional rate. But what is worrying is the share of public transport. It has decreased from 4.18 per cent in 1971 to 0.62 per cent in 2019.[3]

Since private vehicles growth is more, we examined the motorization level (total registered vehicles (vehicles to 1,000 persons) in Figure 3.3. The city tops with the highest number of two wheelers in India. We can see that, the two-wheeler rate has doubled from 209 in 2001 to 454 in 2019. The total vehicles in Figure 3.3 include all registered vehicles (private, public, and goods vehicles).

In the case of cars, it has increased almost three times from 40 cars per thousand persons to 125 in the same period. This indicates the pressure of private vehicles on city's road.[4] Now, let's examine the status of road network in the city.

3.2.2 *Road Network of the City*

Bengaluru has grown into a radial city with nine road corridors forming the principal radial arms, with concentric orbital corridors. NH-7, NH-4 (part of North–South Corridor and Golden Quadrilateral, respectively), and NH-209 pass through Bengaluru forming five important radial roads within

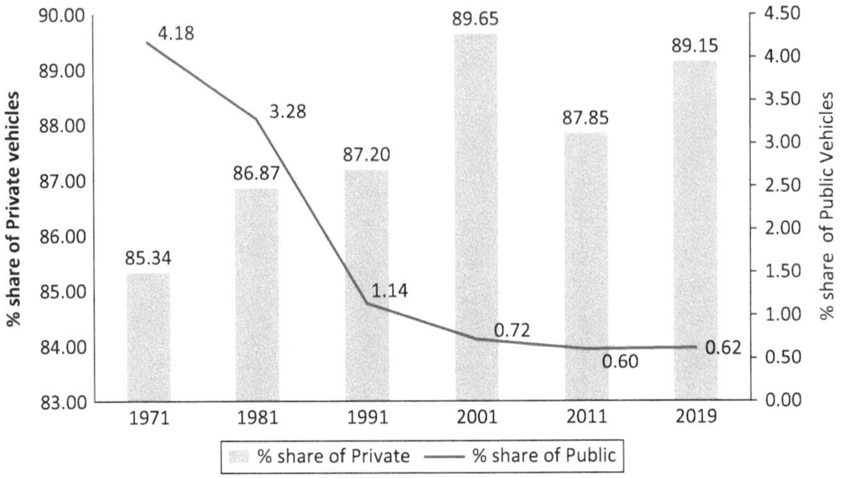

Figure 3.2 Share of Different Transport Mode to Total Vehicular Population.

Source: RTO, Bengaluru.

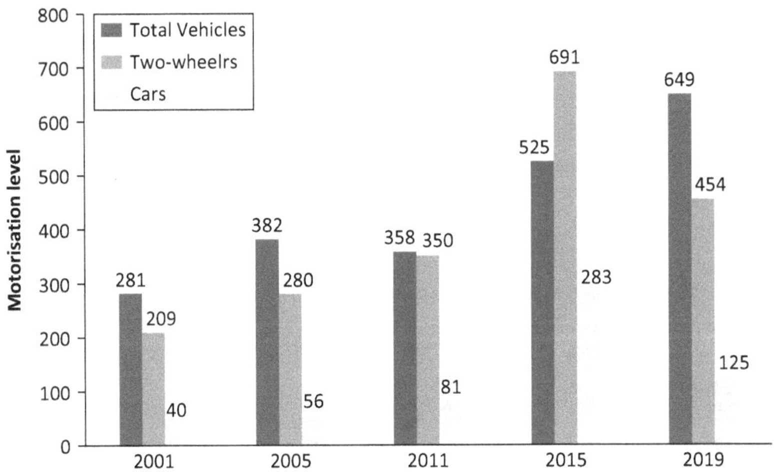

Figure 3.3 Motorization Level in Bengaluru City.

Source: Census Karnataka, RTO Bengaluru.

the Bengaluru Metropolitan Area. Bengaluru has major arterial roads such as Mysore Road, Kanakapura Road, Bannerghatta Road, Magadi Road, and Sarjapura Road, which connect Bengaluru City to other rural areas. Developed as a radial town, Bengaluru does not have a strong circumferential

Table 3.1 Road infrastructure in the city

Year	*Per capita road length (kms per 1,000 population)*
1971	0.937
1981	0.543
1991	0.402
2001	0.357
2011	0.234
2018	0.239

Source: Authors' analysis based on Census Karnataka, RTO Bengaluru, BMR-RMP (2016).

road system, except for the Outer Ring Road (ORR), despite development of the intervening space between the corridors (DULT, 2008).

The primary network, 500–600 kms out of the total road length of 3,000 kms (10,200 kms including other road types like flyovers), includes 10 state and/or national roads and most of them are radial. An ORR (62 km, completed in 2002) plays little role in urban transport, carrying mainly the long-distance traffic. An Intermediate Ring has been constructed in fragments (e.g., south-east between Koramangala and Airport Road). The road network in the city is underdeveloped in terms of size, structure, continuity, and connectivity. The city roads were laid out in the 1940s when Bengaluru had a population of less than half a million. The land development process preceded motorization, and in fact, inhibited the later. The primary roads (ORR and Bengaluru–Mysore Toll Road) are less than 25-metre wide.

It is clear from Table 3.1 that the city's road length is decreasing over the decades. The per capita road length, which was 0.937 kms per 1,000 population in 1971, has reduced to 0.239 kms by 2018, indicating the staggering growth in road length to accommodate the growing demand.

Another dimension of traffic congestion is related to its environmental impacts in the form of air pollution.

3.2.3 Vehicular Air Pollution in the City

Among all the major metropolitan cities of India, Bengaluru is the only city where vehicular exhaust is the major source of air pollution. Nearly 48 per cent of $PM_{2.5}$ in the core area of the city is contributed from vehicular emissions (Auto Fuel Policy, 2014; TERI, 2015). Whereas in other cities like Delhi, domestic sources contribute 47 per cent of air pollution followed by vehicular emission by 22 per cent (Auto Fuel Policy, 2014). This has motivated us to examine the relationship between $PM_{2.5}$ and vehicular population statistically. Figure 3.4 plots the average $PM_{2.5}$ concentration in the city with the vehicular population for 2001 to 2019.

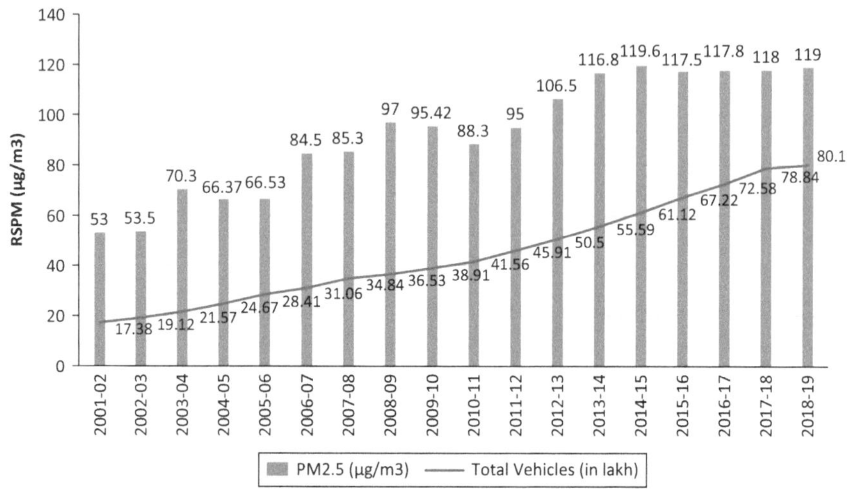

Figure 3.4 $PM_{2.5}$ and Vehicular Population in Bengaluru.

Source: KSPCB and Transport Department of Karnataka Annual Reports from 2001 to 2018.

With the annual growth of vehicular population by 11 per cent from 2001 to 2019, the $PM_{2.5}$ level is increasing at 3.8 per cent annually. The $PM_{2.5}$ level has crossed the national standard of 60 µg/m^3 after 2002–2003. Though graphical representation clearly indicating the positive association among the variables, this needs to be tested theoretically and empirically.

Though they are no well-defined theories which establish the connection between the vehicular growth on PM, we can derive some insights from Engles' theory that as the economy grows, the pollution will also increase. Owing to this, the book makes an important contribution by analyzing the impact of vehicular growth on air pollution of the city using time-series econometric analysis.

3.2.4 *Relationship between $PM_{2.5}$ and Vehicular Population: Time-Series Econometric Analysis*

Equation (3.1) is specified to know the relationship between the $PM_{2.5}$ (in µg/m^3), vehicular population (in million) (vhcl), private vehicle kilometre travelled[5] (vkt), and metro ridership (metro) using their monthly data from May 2016 to August 2019[6]:

$$\ln(PM_{2.5t}) = \beta_0 + \beta_1 \ln(vhcl) + \beta_2 \ln(vkt) + \beta_3(metro) + u_t \quad (3.1)$$

ln is the natural logarithmic form to linearize the series. Vehicular population data are collected from Bengaluru regional transport office (RTO), VKT is estimated based on IRC:100 (1990) guidelines[7] and metro ridership data are obtained from BMRCL (Bengaluru Metro Rail Corporation Ltd.). β_0 is the constant term; β_1, β_2, and β_3 are the long-run elasticities of $PM_{2.5}$ with respect to vhcl, vkt, and metro, respectively.

Similar to the model in Chapter 2, even this data is in time-series pattern. Hence, we follow the stationarity and causality test. For stationarity, Augmented Dickey–Fuller (ADF) and Philip Perron (PP) tests are conducted. The result indicates that vhcl and metro variable are stationary at first difference (I(1)) and PM and vkt are stationary at level (I(0)). Since the model is of mixed order (as explained in Chapter 2), we have adopted ARDL model to test and examine the long run cointegration. The long run equation for the model is provided in Equation (3.2).

$$\begin{aligned}
&\Delta \ln(pm2.5_t) = \\
&\beta_0 \sum_{i=1}^{q} \beta_{1i} \Delta \ln(pm2.5_{t-i}) + \\
&\sum_{i=1}^{q} \beta_{2i} \Delta \ln(vhcl_{t-i}) + \sum_{i=1}^{q} \beta_{3i} \Delta \ln(vkt_{t-i}) \\
&+ \sum_{i=1}^{q} \beta_{4i} \Delta(metro_{t-i}) + \beta_5 \ln(pm2.5_{t-1}) + \beta_6 \ln(vhcl_{t-1}) \\
&+ \beta_7 \ln(vkt_{t-1}) + \beta_8 (metro_{t-1}) + u_{ti}
\end{aligned} \tag{3.2}$$

Where Δ is the first difference operator, q is optimal lag length, β_0 is constant β_1, β_2, β_3, and β_4 represent short-run dynamics of the model, and β_5, β_6, β_7, and β_8 are long-run elasticities. ARDL model of co-integrating vector is reparametrized into Error Correction Mechanism (ECM). The error correction model for Equation (3.2) can be written as Equation (3.3).

$$\begin{aligned}
\Delta \text{lnpm2.5}_t = {} & a_{10} + a_{11}[\text{lnpm2.5}_{t-1} - b_{11}\text{lnvhcl}_{t-1} - b_{12}\text{lnvkt}_{t-1} \\
& - b_{13}\text{metro}_{t-1}] + \gamma_{11}\Delta\text{lnpm2.5}_{t-i} + \gamma_{12}\Delta\text{lnvhcl}_{t-i} \\
& + \gamma_{13}\text{'' lnvkt}_{t-i} + \gamma_{14}\Delta\text{metro}_{t-i} + \varepsilon_{ti}
\end{aligned} \tag{3.3}$$

The coefficient a_{11} indicates the speed of adjustment to equilibrium and its corresponding value in the bracket is the error correction term. The γ coefficient indicates the short-term relation. For the cointegration, these coefficients must be significantly different from zero and estimates of them must not be too large (it must lie between 0 and −1). In order to find out the long-run relationship, Bound F-test on Equation (3.2) is conducted with two bounds, i.e., lower and upper bound.

H_0 (null hypothesis) – there is no cointegration among variables.

Table 3.2 Short- and long-term estimates of the model long-term estimates

Regressor	*Coefficient*	*t-stat*
Constant	−39.98[b]	1.62
$Ln(vhcl_t)$	0.271[a]	1.8
$Ln(vkt_t)$	0.110[b]	0.7
Metro	−0.309[a]	−1.93

With respect to the lag length, SIC and AIC are used to select the optimal lag length of variables, which gives the optimal lag length as one. Since the data is in the monthly series, we expect the impact will be captured within a month.

3.2.5 Results and Discussion

The short-run and long-run results of the model are given in Table 3.2. The result indicates that, the variables under consideration have a positive impact on $PM_{2.5}$. This means, 1 per cent increase in total vehicular population will increase the $PM_{2.5}$ level in the city by 27.1 per cent, whereas vehicle kilometre travel will increase $PM_{2.5}$ level by 11 per cent. An important finding is related to the metro variable. One unit increase in the metro ridership decreases the $PM_{2.5}$ pollution level by 30.9 per cent. This indicates that the use of metro trains will significantly reduce the $PM_{2.5}$ pollution and improve the city's air quality. The results are in tune with the reports of KSPCB (2001–2018).

Short-term estimates[d]

$$\Delta\ln(pm2.5_t) = \underset{(-4.64)}{-0.55EC^{a}} + \underset{(1.9)}{0.39\,\Delta\ln(PM_{2.5}(-1))^{a}} + \underset{(1.02)}{1.51\Delta\ln(vhcl(-1))^{a}} + \underset{(0.83)}{0.06\Delta\ln(vkt(-1))^{a}} - \underset{(-2.12)}{0.17metro^{a}}$$

$R^2 = 0.57$; Adj. $R^2 = 0.65$.

[a]Significant at 1 per cent level; [b]Significant at 5 per cent level; [c]Significant at 10 per cent level; [d]t-values are in parenthesis.

The short-run error correction (EC) term is negative and significant, indicating the existence of cointegration among the variables. The speed of adjustment is 0.55, suggesting that nearly 55 per cent of disequilibrium is corrected within a month. The model is verified with the F-statistics where the computed F-statistics (7.21) is above critical upper bound I (1) value (3.3). According to Pesaran and Pesaran (1997) and Pesaran et al. (2001), this confirms that the variables have long-run relationships and thereby rejects the null hypothesis.

The model is tested for stability using CUSUM and CUSUMSQ and Multicollinearity, Heteroskedasticity, and normality tests. The result indicates that the model is structurally stable and reliable (refer to Appendixes 3.1 and 3.2).

With the empirical evidence on the impact of vehicular population on air quality, the book proceeds to examine the major factors contributing to traffic congestion in the city. This section gives a micro-level picture of the problem. Even similar factors are found in other metro cities of the country.

3.3 Factors Affecting the Traffic Congestion in Bengaluru

Traffic congestion is affected by multitudinal factors. These factors are broadly classified into economic, social, institutional, technical, and governance factors.

a. **Economic Factors:** Economic factors act as vital causes of congestion in any city, the same holds true for Bengaluru.

- **Urbanization:** The population of the city is growing at a rate of 46.68 per cent in the past decade (2001–2011). It can be attributed that the main cause is due to the IT sector in the city, which is offering higher employment opportunities (Census, 2011).
- **Workforce participation** in Bengaluru was 29.83 per cent in 1981, which increased to 36 per cent in 2011 and projected to increase to 38 per cent in 2031 (Census, 2011). As of 2011, 45 per cent of the total population is working population in Bengaluru. Such high working force tends to have a positive impact on motorization.
- **Income growth:** The city's per capita income is growing at the rate of 14 per cent from 2001 to 2019; this is much higher than the country's 6.8 per cent. Such growth in income is proved to have a positive impact on the growth of the vehicles.
- **Vehicular growth:** The main cause of congestion is private vehicular growth, which is growing at 11 per cent per annum during 2001–2019 in Bengaluru.
- **Road capacity:** Major roads of Bengaluru like Nrupatunga road, KG road, MG road, Chord Road, Richmond Road, Puttanna Chetty Road, and Sankey Road are operating above their capacity during peak hours (BTP, 2015), indicating severe congestion issues. Further, according to the India Mobility Final report by Global Mobility Monitor Network (2008), the road density in Bengaluru is only 8.2 km per sq. km, which is almost one-third of the national capital (21.6 km per sq. km).

b. **Social Factors:** Education and gender are key social factors of traffic congestion. Generally, these factors influence the travel mode choice. Even we examined the same where, the probability of male opting private transport is higher than the female. In case of education, as the level of education increases, people may prefer to travel in own vehicles. This surely accentuates the traffic congestion (results are provided in Section 3.5.3 in this chapter).

c. **Institutional or Behavioural Factors:** Institutional factors of traffic congestion are related to the commuter behaviour and institutional working pattern in the city. Some of the institutional factors which are apparent in the city are:

- **Preference to Public Transport:** It is shocking to observe that, commuters in the city are rapidly shifting from public transport to private mode. For instance, the daily ridership in the city's BMTC (Bengaluru Metropolitan Transport Corporation) bus was around 51.3 lakh in 2014–2015, which has drastically decreased to 35.8 lakh in 2018–2019 (BMTC, 2019). On the contrary, the private vehicles (two-wheelers and cars) have increased from 49.2 lakhs to 85.6 lakh in the same period, showing a 44.6 per cent increase. This has led to severe pressure on the road causing the worst form of traffic congestion in the city.
- **Parking Patterns:** Irrational parking in the city has been identified as the major cause of traffic congestion by the traffic police department (BTP, 2016). This reduces the right of way for the vehicles on road.
- **Bad Reaches:** BBMP (2019) identified that in 2017 there are around 12,926 sq mts of bad reaches, 5,360 sq mts potholes in Bengaluru. This causes not only traffic congestion but also severe accidents (leading to death).
- **Time of Travel:** The standard work time followed by many companies in the city has created peak hour congestion. As travelling for the work/school induces more demand for vehicles on the road leading to traffic congestion.
- The **inner core road network** of the city is choked due to lack of proper connectivity and legibility. Although the ring roads can take the increased volume of traffic, people tend to use the major roads as a thoroughfare, as the ring road is about 8 kms away from the city centre. Travelling this extra distance is considered as a burden by the commuters both in terms of time and cost. Though recently Metro trains are introduced, it is still at its infancy stage to yield desired benefits.

c. **Technical Factors:** The technical factors include certain technical errors in the form of improper signals operating in major junctions of the road and unscientific humps in the road. Even form the field survey it is observed that, out of 15 junctions, 13 junctions do not have a yellow light indication in the traffic signals. These issues have intensified traffic congestion in the city.

d. **Governance Factors:** Non-obeyance of traffic rules by the public created hoax in the roadway. There are around 44,03,985 cases booked by Bangalore Traffic Police (BTP, 2018) for non-obeyance of traffic rules. Further, there is lack of proper pedestrian path and slow-moving vehicles (like loaded lorries, tractors, and goods vehicles) are intensifying the congestion in the city.

  The analysis provided so far has highlighted the issue of traffic congestion in the city with its impact on both the economy and environment. This description may not attract policymakers to address the issue unless the ill effects are quantified. As there is dearth of secondary data for the city, primary survey is conducted. The following section provides the details of the survey and sample.

3.4 Description of the Study Area and Data

The quantification of the economic cost of traffic congestion needs a systematic and regular collection of traffic-flow data. Since such information is not available, we relied on field surveys. The survey is undertaken from December 2018 to February 2019. The city falls under Bengaluru Urban District (BUD) which consists of four taluks, namely, Bengaluru North, South, East, and Anekal Taluk (Map 3.3). The metropolitan region of Bengaluru is under the municipal corporation jurisdiction called BBMP (Bruhat Bengaluru Mahanagara Palike), which is considered as the study area.

BBMP area serves as the economic powerhouse of the region as well as the State. The population in the core city has grown 1.5 times in the last 10 years and projections indicate that from around six million in 2001, it will grow to 14.4 million in 2031 (BMR-RMP, 2016). Between 2001 and 2021, Bengaluru's household income has increased at an average of almost 14 per cent per year. The ever-growing disposable income and easy availability of loan have increased the vehicular ownership causing gridlocks in traffic movement.

To quantify the impacts of traffic congestion in the city, few sample locations are identified as representatives of the city's traffic situation. For the selection of such locations, we relied on the Revised Master Plan (RMP) report 2031 (2016), which has classified the 198 wards of BBMP into 23 planning districts (PD)[8].

As the city is growing in concentric pattern, we have classified it into four zones namely central business district (CBD), adjacent CBD, inner periphery, and periphery (Table 3.3).

Table 3.3 Classification of study zones

Name of the zone	*Name of the wards*
Central business district (CBD)	Jayamahal, Ulsoor, Vasanth Nagar, Gandhi Nagar, Okalipuram, Dayanand Nagar, Prakash Nagar, Sampanigara, Cottonpet, K.R.Market
Adjacent CBD	Indiranagar, Koramangala, Jayanagar, Rajajinagar, Malleshwaram
Inner peripheral zone	HSR Layout, Yeshwanthpur, RT Nagar, Hebbal, Thanisandra-Nagawara, Katriguppe
Peripheral zone	Banaswadi, KR Puram, Whitefield, Belanduru, Hulimavu, BTM Gottigere, Nagarbhavi-Peenya, Jalahalli, Yelhanka

Source: Classification based on BMR-RMP, 2016.

Table 3.4 Land-use and demographic details of the study zones

Zone	*Total Area (km^2)*	*Habited area (km^2)*	*Commercial area (% to habited area)*	*Residential area (% to habited area)*	*Population density (person/ km^2)*
CBD	27.74	22.33	26.2	25.3	46,505
Adjacent CBD	149.64	106.05	11.3	51.1	25,512
Inner periphery	214.07	120.43	8.5	49.1	24,531
Peripheral Zone	232.18	104.82	8.3	42.4	16,845
BBMP[11]	**623.63**	**353.64**	**9.8**	**48.1**	**23,935**

Source: Classification based on BMR-RMP, 2016 & Census, 2011.

The traditional and major commercial setups are at the centre forming the central business district (CBD), and residential and semi-commercial areas at the adjacent of the CBD. IT and IT-related firms established at the inner periphery and a few industries are found in peripheral zones. These zones classified in Table 3.5 are based on the major activities in each PD rather than the population of the PD[9] to cover the entire jurisdictional limit of BBMP.

In term of land use (Table 3.4), the CBD has been the commercial centre of the city with 26.2 per cent of its habited area[10] occupied by commercial setups (like Pete area of the city with 18 BBMP wards). In this zone, we can observe high population density. The adjacent CBD forms the residential periphery to the CBD, which occupies almost 51 per cent of the habited area and 11.3 per cent by the commercial establishments. This indicates that the city's growth can be identified as Thünen's (1826) city formation model. The third zone of the study is referred to as the inner periphery, which forms the IT zone of the city. Even in this zone, residential setups are higher than (49 per cent) than the commercial establishment (8.5 per cent). The periphery zone of the city forms the BBMP jurisdictional limits (as per Census, 2011)

Table 3.5 Details of the sample junctions of the study

Zone	*Zones*	*Study junctions*	*Sample size*
1	CBD	Corporation Circle, Hudson Circle, KR circle	107
2	Adjacent CBD	Trinity circle, Richmond circle, Navarang junction, Oklipuram signal	106
3	Inner Periphery	Magadi Road, Mekri circle, Sony world, Silk Board	108
4	Periphery	BEL circle, Hebbal flyover, KR Puram junction (Tin factory), Marathhalli bridge signal	106
Total			**427**

Source: Author.

and the impact of city's expansion can be observed from this zone. This zone is not only growing with commercial establishments, but there is an equal growth in residential areas. These are causing congestion in the area as it also connects to the interstate highways.

In terms of population growth, as per Census 2011, the CBD is experiencing negative growth rate. On the other hand, inner periphery and peripheral areas are experiencing more than 80 per cent increase in population.

In these zones, there are certain key junctions which are operating beyond their capacity. Due to commercial operations spreading in the peripheral areas and administration activities concentrated in CBD, traffic congestion is observed in the entire city. Hence, it is important to identify those traffic junctions for the quantification. In the next section, we provide the details on the selection of traffic junction and the details on the sample data.

3.4.1 Selection and Description of Traffic Junctions for the Study

The identification of traffic junction is mainly based on the report by Directorate of Urban Land Transport (DULT)'s 'Bangalore Mobility Indicators' (2011) and findings of sub-group on Traffic of the Vision Group and Bangalore Traffic Police (BTP) report (2016). These reports identified that, out of 388 signalized junctions in the city, nearly 15 traffic junctions are operating beyond their capacity (volume-to-capacity ratio > 1). In these junctions, traffic stream stays more than three minutes. This means signal-cycle failure and heavy congestion. These junctions are taken as study junctions that are placed as per the zonal classification (refer to Table 3.5).

In Zone 1, i.e., Central Business District of Bengaluru, three major junctions are identified, namely, Hudson circle, Corporation circle, and KR circle. These junctions are in the heart of the city. They connect the main administrative and commercial centres. Especially Corporation circle carries heavy traffic as it connects major commercial hubs like KR market from the northern part of the city. Zone 2 includes junctions like Trinity circle, Richmond circle, Navarang signal, and Oklipuram signal, which connect the business zones of the city. Mainly Trinity and Richmond circle are the main junctions which carry heavy business traffic of the city. Zone 1 and 2 are of importance as these zones are equipped with metro trains.

In Zone 3, major junctions identified are Sony world, Magadi road toll gate, Mekri circle, and Silk board flyover signal. With major MNCs situated in these areas like Electronic City and Koramangala and also connecting to the outer ring road, these junctions carry peak-hour traffic. An infamous junction viz., Silk Board signal connects major IT companies and also carries heavy commercial traffic as it is the main junction through which the city is connected to the interstate highway (Tamil Nadu). Zone 4 belongs to the periphery area of Bengaluru which forms the final jurisdiction limit of BBMP. The traffic movement in this area has become a matter of concern in recent years due to the expansion of city limits. Major junctions of this zone are Hebbal flyover signal, KR Puram signal (Tin factory), BEL circle, and Yeshwanthpur signal.

3.4.2 Sampling Technique and the Sample Size

To quantify the traffic congestion costs, regularity of travel is important. Hence, we considered recurrent congestion (regular peak-hour congestion) and interviewed working commuters (due to regularity of their travel). To have a representative sample size, an average of 100 samples is taken from each zone by giving equal importance to different occupational levels.[12] The details of the selected junctions and sample size are provided in Table 3.5.

A total sample of 445 respondents (commuters) has been collected using a stratified random sampling technique (Figure 3.5). Out of 445, 427

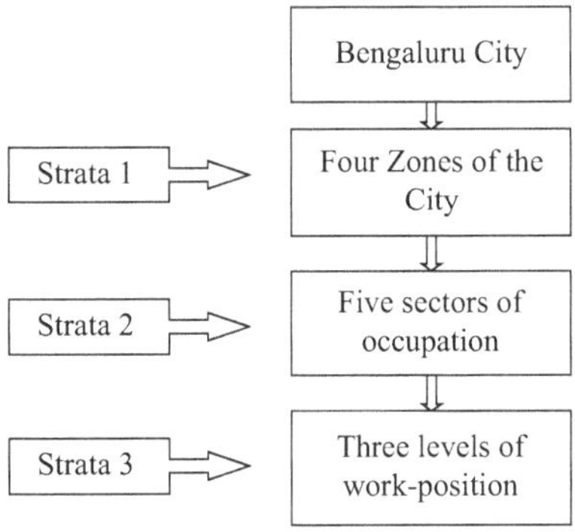

Figure 3.5 Different Strata of Sampling.

Source: Author

responses are considered, and the rest 18 are unanswered or semi-filled questionnaires.

Work-place interviews are conducted with structured questionnaires. The questionnaire consisted of five main parts. Part A has collected the information regarding the socio-economic and demographic characteristics of the sample; Part B collected the travel details of the respondents; the health and productivity information of the respondents are collected in Part C; Part D has obtained the information regarding the status and opinion of the respondents regarding the air quality of city and contribution of vehicular emissions to the air pollution. Lastly, Part E has elicited the willingness to pay for the reduced traffic-related air pollution, which reduces the related mortality.

3.5 Demographic, Economic, and Travel Profile of the Sample

The data on the travel pattern of commuters, mode choice, time of travel, and their socio-economic information are collected. These details form the basis for quantification. This section elaborates them in detail.

3.5.1 Demographic Profile of the Respondents

The demographic profile includes gender, marital status, age, and educational status of the respondents. Among the total respondents (427), 65 per cent of them are male and rest are female. In terms of age, the majority of respondents belong to the age group of 26–35 years (34%) and 36–45 years (22%). This includes almost 56 per cent of the respondents, belonging to the young and middle age groups. Age is an important demographic variable as it determines vehicular ownership.

Education is yet another variable that determines the travel pattern of the respondents. Figure 3.6 provides the educational status of the sample, where nearly 75 per cent of the respondents belong to graduates and above category.

3.5.2 Economic Profile of the Respondents

The economic profile of the study area includes the income level and vehicular ownership of the respondents. The information on income provided in Figure 3.7 is recorded as specified by the respondents (monthly income) from their occupation.

The majority of the respondents (44.3%) belong to the income group of Rs. 15,001–Rs. 35,000 per month as on 2018–2019. Around 21.6 per cent of the respondents belong to the income group of Rs. 35,001–55,000 and 20 per cent belong to less than Rs. 15,000 per month. The average income of the sample is Rs. 34,952/month.

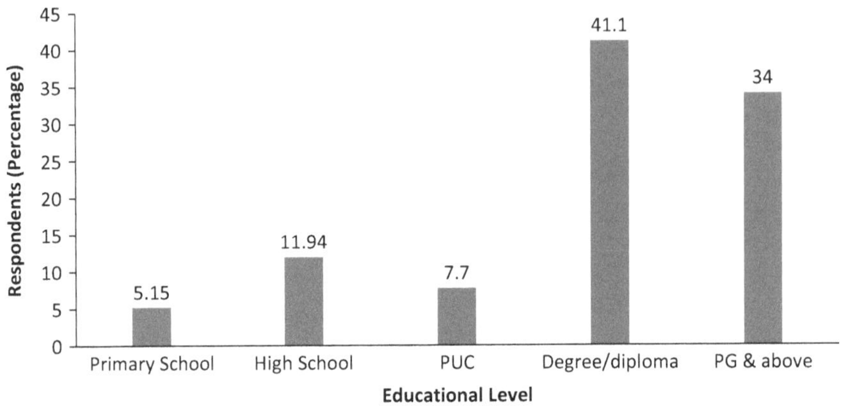

Figure 3.6 Educational Status among the Respondents.

Source: Primary Data.

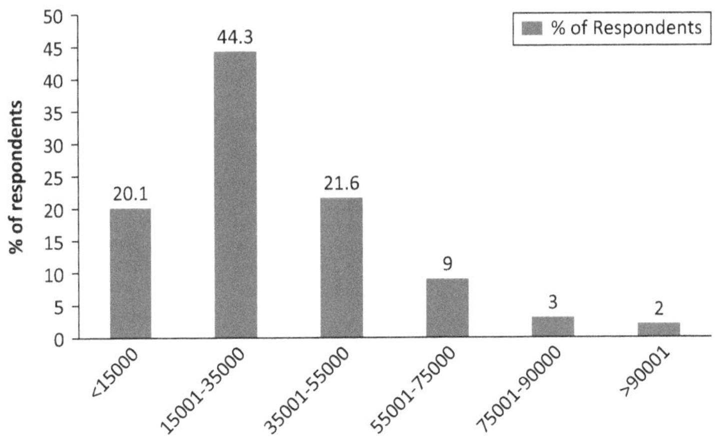

Figure 3.7 Income level of the Respondents (Rs. per month).

Source: Primary data.

3.5.3 *Travel Profile of the Study Area*

The travel details provide key input in the quantification model. The modal choice, distance travelled, and junction delay information will provide information regarding the travel choice and pattern in the sample.

3.5.3.1 *Trip Length Information*

The distance travelled data will provide the information regarding the trip length from origin to destination. We collected the data on the working commuters of the city, the distance travelled would reveal the information regarding the trip length from home to workplace or vice versa.

The average distance travelled by the commuters in the city is around 14.7 kms per day (one-way). That means, the average trip length in a day would be 29.4 kms. If we compare this result to the Bangalore Mobility indicator report (DULT, 2011) (11 kms), we can see a leaping increase in the trip length. The commuters in the city are making longer trips due to uncontrolled expansion of the city.

The description of commuters' profile would give some idea on their travel behaviour. But in transport studies, their modal choice analysis becomes integral analysis. We also make an important analysis of this for an Indian city. This will guide the urban planners of developing countries with respect to the behavioural aspect.

3.5.3.2 *Modal Choice Distribution*

The model choice includes the choice of respondents between private mode of transport and the public mode of transport. This data will assist in predicting the share of each type of mode dominating the trip pattern in the city. Further, we can also understand the factors influencing their travel mode choice. In our data, 63.5 per cent of them use private mode of transport, whereas 36.5 per cent are dependent on a public mode of transportation. In all four zones, similar ratios are found.

Generally, travel demand models use the mode choice for forecasting the travel demand. In our study, we make an important analysis on the understanding of the behavioural aspect of commuters. This will provide key insights on how the travel behaviour has a significant impact on the economy and the environment.

Research studies on travel mode choice analysis can be traced back to McFadden's (1974). He used binary logit model to know the mode choice between automobile and bus services for a sample of 160. The study found that the socio-economic variables like income, gender, and walk time to transit services are the key variables in determining the modal choice of the commuters. Similar results are found by Arasan et al. (1996). Thompson-Graves et al. (2006) examined the trip characteristics, land use, and urban design as factors to influence the mode-choice.

Various studies (Camilleri, 2007; Perry, 1997) have found that demographic factors also influence mode choice significantly. Racca and Ratledge

(2004) reported in their project study on Delware, that gender, income, race, age, household size, trip purpose, and parking space significantly influence the mode choice. Many studies found the positive impact of socio-economic factors like gender, education, and income on the modal choice determination (Chatterjee, 2011; Steg et al., 2001; Murray et al., 2011).

An interesting study by Tyrinopoulos and Antoniou (2013) highlights the factors affecting the mode choice and reasons that discourage the use of public transportation services. By using probit and structural equations, the study revealed that female respondents preferred public transport than male respondents. Major factor discouraging the use of public transport is found to be over-crowding in public transit rather than high fare in Greece (Municipality of Kalamaria). Even in studies by Alvinsyah and Nainggolan (2005) in Jakarta, Thamizh Arasan and Vedagiri (2011) and Marikowa et al. (2003) study in Japan found that female preferred the public transit than the male. In an Indian study by Srinivasan et al. (2007) who analyzed the mode-choice determinants for vehicle type with respect to socio-economic variables in Chennai city. In the recent study by Parola et al. (2018), who examined the influence of age and gender in determining the public transit services on a pooled sample of 86,958 in Anglo countries concluded that the use of public transit increases with age and female favour public transportation than the male.

As there are no such studies found on Bengaluru, we made an important contribution to literature by examining the mode choice analysis. Based on the theoretical literature, we specify Eq (3.4) for the model.

$$Mode_{choice} = \beta_0 gen + \beta_1 age + \beta_2 edu + \beta_3 inc + \beta_4 TTR + \beta_5 TD + \beta_6 Dis + \mu \qquad (3.4)$$

As the mode-choice variable is a nominal dependent variable with more than two categories, multinomial logit regression is used to examine which of the independent variables significantly predict the modal choice of commuters in the city. The independent variables are chosen based on the review of literature. The descriptions of the variables are provided in Table 3.6.

The likelihood ratio (LR) from chi-square test provides the result regarding the fit of the model compared with the complete set of predictors with an intercept only or null model. Based on LR test, we can say that the model containing the full set of predictors represents a significant improvement in fit relative to a null model (LR $X^2(14) = 245.67$, $\rho<.001$). It can be inferred that at least one population slope is non-zero. The pseudo R^2 (called McFadden's pseudo R^2)[13] can be considered as an index of the proportionate improvement in model fit relative to the null model (Pituch & Stevens, 2016). In the model pseudo R^2 is 0.2844, which can be interpreted as the full model containing all the predictors represents 28.44 per cent improvement in fit relative to the null model.

Table 3.6 Description of the variables of modal choice analysis

Variables	*Description*
Mode_choice	Mode preferences of the respondents Public transport = 0 (Base-line category) Two-wheelers = 1 Cars = 2
Gender (*gen*)	Sex of the respondents Male = 1 Female = 0
Age	Age of the respondents in years
Edu	The education of the respondents (in years of education)
Income (*inc*)	Monthly income of the respondents (in Rs.)
Dis	Distance to the nearest transit station (bus stop or metro station) (in kms)
TTR	Total time taken to travel from origin to destination (in kms)
TD	Total delay due to traffic congestion (in minutes)

Table 3.7 Results on MNL for two-wheeler users vs public transport users

Predictors	*Coef.*	*SE*	*RRR*	*SE*
Gender	0.529[a]	0.247	1.731[a]	0.431
Age	0.019[b]	0.015	1.019[b]	0.015
Education	0.156[a]	0.050	1.172[a]	0.058
Income	0.080	0.030	1.045	0.001
Traffic delay	0.050[a]	0.008	1.048[a]	0.009
Total travel time	−0.023[a]	0.005	0.969[a]	0.006
Distance to transit	1.035[a]	0.240	1.039[a]	0.200
Constant	−3.890[a]	0.991	–	–

Source: Authors estimation. Level of significance at 1 and 5 per cent are represented by [a] and [b], respectively.

For the dependent variable, commuters using public transport are considered as the base category (coded as 0), which do not take any coefficients or tests; and the comparison group will be two-wheeler users (coded as 1) and car users (coded as 2). Table 3.7 provides the results of MNL for the probability of choosing public transport (baseline category) as against two-wheeler (i.e., comparison group).

Among the independent variables, socio-economic variables viz., age, gender, and education have positive and significant influence on the dependent variable. As age or education increases, there is a higher probability of commuters choosing two-wheeler over public transport. In case of gender, males are more likely than females to opt for two-wheeler for their daily commute. In the case of income, the result is showing insignificant influence. Among

Table 3.8 Results on MNL for car users vs public transport users

Predictors	*Coef.*	*SE*	*RRR*	*SE*
Gender	1.258[b]	0.451	3.510[a]	1.594
Education	0.616[a]	0.191	1.864[a]	0.358
Age	0.060[a]	0.027	1.061[a]	0.024
Income	0.006[a]	0.002	1.023[a]	0.001
Traffic delay	0.485[a]	0.011	1.047[a]	0.119
Total travel time	−0.035[a]	0.007	0.964[a]	0.008
Distance to transit	1.270[a]	0.270	1.002[a]	0.297
Constant	−17.20[a]	4.146	–	–

Source: Authors estimation. Level of significance at 1% and 5% are represented by [a] and [b], respectively.

the travel related variables, traffic delay, and distance to transit are found to be positive and significant. This indicates that as traffic delay increases or if there is longer distance to nearest transit stop, probability of commuters opting two-wheeler is high as against the public transport. In the case of total travel time, the model is showing negative influence. This indicates that the commuters in the city with longer distance to travel have lesser chance of choosing two-wheeler and opt public transport for their daily commute. This result is in line with studies like McFadden, 1974, Chatterjee, 2011; Steg et al., 2001; Murray et al., 2011; Camilleri, 2007; Perry, 1997.

For the second comparison group, i.e., car users (coded as 2), the result of the predictors are provided in Table 3.8. As found with the two-wheelers, even the predictors for the car users show similar results. The gender, age, and education predictors in the model are found to be positive and significant.

In the case of 'income' predictor, the variable is found to be positive and significant in indicating that commuters with higher income have higher chance of opting cars for their daily commute and of lower chance of choosing public transport as compared to commuters with lower income levels.

The travel-related predictors like 'travel time', 'distance to transit', and 'traffic delay' have similar results in the case of car users as with the two-wheelers. As traffic delay and distance to transit increases, the probability of commuters choosing car against public transport will also increase. As found with two-wheelers, the total travel time predictor is found to be significant and has a negative influence. This highlights that if the travel time increases, the probability of commuters choosing public transport increases against cars.

3.5.4 *Relative Risk Ratio (RRR) Analysis and Inference from the Result*

In the context of logistic regression, relative risk ratio (RRR) involves a comparison of two groups in terms of risk or likelihood of a given outcome. It provides a ratio of the probability (risk) of a case falling into a comparison group to the probability of the case belonging to the baseline group (Osborne, 2015). Osborne (2015) and Sedgwick (2014) pointed out that the odds ratio overestimates the relative risk. RRR gives the change in the relative risk per unit increase on an independent variable.

In the case of our model, it can be understood that the relative risk ratio of gender in case of both car and two-wheelers (private transport) is greater than one, indicating the male (coded as 1) are at greater probability of opting private vehicles (1.7 in case of two-wheeler and 3.5 in case of cars) and at a lesser probability of choosing public transport as compared to the female. This means female commuters are found to choose a more sustainable mode of transportation in the city. In the case of age, RRR is greater than one (1.01: two-wheeler; 1.8: cars). This highlights that as age increases the probability of choosing private vehicles also increases. The economic variable: 'income', though has a positive impact but is significant only for the comparison category of cars than for two-wheelers. This suggests the income is a significant variable for the commuters to opt for cars than the two-wheelers.

The RRR of traffic delay (1.04-two-wheelers and cars) and distance to transit (1.03-two-wheelers and 1.0 for car) indicates that commuters with longer traffic delays and distance to transit are more likely to opt for private transport and have less probability of choosing public transportation as their mode-choice. This result highlights the paradoxical situation in the city where private vehicles are not only the victims of traffic congestion but also the cause of the same. In the case of the RRR of total travel time, the result is quite interesting. The RRR for total travel time is less than one in case of both the modes ($0.96 < 1$). This means for one unit increase in total travel time, the probability of choosing private vehicle will decrease, and the likelihood of opting public transport would increase. This result suggests that the city should implement a comprehensive public transport policy which would aim at increasing the frequency and accessibility of transportation.

The MNL result brought key input for further analysis. The result highlighted that economic, social, and institutional factors are affecting the mode choice significantly. Commuters prefer private transport for varied reasons. The higher use of private vehicles tends to accentuate traffic congestion. With this information, it can be inferred that in the city the economic costs of traffic congestion is mainly due to private transport and the public transport users are the sufferers of this burden. The next chapter attempts to quantify the economic cost of traffic congestion for both private and public transport users.

3.6 Conclusion

The chapter provided an elaborate description of the study area with details on the geographical location of the sample junctions, the sampling framework and the economic and demographic profile of the respondents.

The chapter examined the factors influencing traffic congestion in the study area. It is found that the vehicular population in the city is highly correlated with the per capita income and urbanization which has led to severe traffic congestion. A key finding of the chapter is related to the impact of this vehicular growth on the air pollution of the city. It is found that personal vehicular ownership increases the $PM_{2.5}$ level considerably, whereas the metro train use will bring down both congestion and pollution in the city.

The average distance travelled by the commuters in the city has doubled from 11 kms/day (DULT, 2011) to 29 kms/day indicating speed of city's expansion. Using logit regression, we provided that there are accessibility issues in public transport in the city. Longer distance to the nearest public transit station tends to increase the private vehicular ownership, which further accentuates the traffic congestion in the city.

Notes

1 Per capita income at constant prices of 2011–2012.
2 Accessed from www.transport.karnataka.gov.in on 10 May 2020.
3 This data does not include the Metro trains.
4 A decrease in the motorization level in 2011 can be linked to post-impact of the recessionary trend in the economy.
5 Though there are other factors like road dust etc., which affect the $PM_{2.5}$ level, the study assumed that they are the result of the vehicular population (TERI, 2015).
6 The data is available from May 2016 to August 2019 in KSPCB.
7 Private vehicle kilometre travelled (VKT) is derived using average trip length and total vehicles called the load factor. Load factor is the average number of distance travelled by a category of vehicle in a day. Load factor for private transport = 15kms/day.
8 The RMP-2031 provides a total of 42 planning districts of which 23 PDs fall under BBMP jurisdiction.
9 Population is not equal in every PD or zone of the BBMP.
10 Habited area includes residential, commercial, industrial, public and semi-public setups, and transport use of land. It excludes vacant land, forest, parks, and lakes area.
11 Except Varthur and Herohalli which are in the outer periphery of BBMP jurisdiction.
12 Different sectors like government, IT, Bank, self employed, and informal sectors are considered. Among them, different levels of work positions from professionals like doctors, lawyers, etc. to salespersons are interviewed. Even the street vendors and garment workers are included in the sample.
13 Though not computed in the same way as R^2 in OLS but can be interpreted as an index of improvement.

References

Alvinsyah, S. S., & Nainggolan, P. T. (2005). Public transport user attitude based on choice model parameter characteristics (case study: Jakarta bus way system). *Journal of Eastern Asia Society for Transportation Studies*, 6, 480–491.

Arasan, V. T., Rangarajan, V. R., & Krishna Rao, K. V. (1996). Trip characteristics of travellers without vehicles. *Journal of Transport Engineering*, *122*(1), 76–81.
Auto Fuel Policy. (2014). Auto fuel vision and vision 2025. Retrieved June 27, 2019, from http://petroleum.nic.in/sites/default/files/autopol.pdfon
BBMP (Bruhat Bengaluru MahanagaraPalike). (2018). Details on road length and maps of the city. www.bbmp.gov.in/annualreports
BBMP (Bruhat Bengaluru MahanagaraPalike). (2019). Status of potholes/road pertaining to BBMP limits. http://bbmp.gov.in/pothole
BMR-RMP. (2016). Bangalore metropolitan region revised plan 2031. BMRDA, Groupe SCE India Pvt. Ltd. http://bmrda.karnataka.gov.in/Documents/Revised%20Structure%20Plan%20Report-ilovepdf-compressed.pdf
BMTC (Bengaluru Metropolitan Transport Corporation). (2017–18). Annual administration report. www.mybmtc.karnataka.gov.in
BMTC (Bengaluru Metropolitan Transport Corporation). (2019). Annual administration report. www.mybmtc.karnataka.gov.in
BTP (Bengaluru Traffic Police). (2015–2018). Traffic violation details. BTP. www.btp.gov.in
Camilleri, E. (2007). Antecedent affecting public service motivation. *Personal Review*, *36*(3), 356–377. https://doi.org/10.1108/00483480710731329
Census of India (2001 [2011]). Population data. http://censusindia.gov.in/
Chatterjee, K. (2011). Modeling dynamics of bus use in a changing travel environment using panel data. *Transportation*, *38*(3), 487–509.
Del Salazan, S., González-Gómez, F., & Guardiola, F. (2015). Willingness to pay to improve urban water supply: The case of Sucre, Bolivia. *Water Policy*, *17*(1), 112–125.
Dewaram, W., Spengler, J. D., & Schwartz, J. (1997). Valuing environmental cost in India: The economy wide impact of environmental degradation. *Environmental Research*, *59*, 362–373.
District Census Report of Karnataka. (2001 [2011]). Population data. www.census2011.co.in›Karnataka›DistrictList
DULT (Directorate of Urban Land Transport). (2008 & 2011). Bangalore urban mobility indicators 2008 and 2010–11, Draft final report, by Urban Mass Transit Company Limited.
Forbes. (2017). Forbes global 2000. *Forbes*. www.forbes.com/global2000/
Global Mobility Report. (2017). https://sustainabledevelopment.un.org/content/documents/2643Global_Mobility_Report_2017.pdf
IBM. (2011). *Frustration rising*. IBM 2011 commuter pain survey. IBM.
JLL (Jones Lang LaSalle). (2020). City momentum index 2020. https://www.jll.co.in/en/trends-and-insights/research/city-momentum-index-2020
Marikowa, T., Yamamoto, Y., Dissanyake, D., Sanko, M., Kurauchi, S., Maesoba, H., Ohashi, S., Tiglao, N., Rubite, C., & Rivera, M. (2003). Travel behavior analysis and its implication to urban transport planning for Asian cities: Case studies in Bangkok, Kuala Lampur, Manila and Nagoya research project, International co-operative Research Activity (ICRA). Nagoya University.
McFadden, D. (1974). The measurement of urban travel demand. *Journal of Public Economics*, *5*, 303–328.
Murray, S. J., Walton, D., & Thomas, J. A. (2011). Attitudes towards public transport in New Zealand. *Transportation*, *37*(6), 915–929.

Osborne, W. J. (2015). *Best practices in logistic regression.* Sage Publishing.

Parola, R. H., Harari, B. M., Herst, L. D., & Prysmakova, P. (2018). Demographic determinants of public service motivation: A meta-analysis of PSM-age and gender relationships. *Public Management Review.* https://doi.org/10.1080/14719037.2018.1550108

Perry, J. (1997). Antecedent of public service motivation. *Journal of Public Administration Research and Theory*, 7(20), 181–197.

Pesaran, H. M., & Pesaran, B. (1997). *Microfit 4.0: Interactive econometric analysis.* Oxford University Press.

Pesaran, H. M., Shin, Y., & Smith, I. R. (2001). Bound testing approaches to the analysis of level relationship. *Journal of Applied Econometrics*, *16*, 289–326.

Pituch, A. K., & Stevens, P. J. (2016). *Applied multivariate statistics for the social sciences: Analysis with SAS and IBM's SPSS.* Routledge.

Racca, P. D., & Ratledge, C. E. (2004). Project report on factors that affect and/or can alter mode choice, prepared for Centre for Applied demography and survey research, University of Delaware, Newark. www.researchgate.net/publication/26990727

Ramachandra, T. V., & Aithal, H. B. (2014). Wetlands: Kidneys of Bangalore's landscape. Retrieved March 25, 2020, from wgbis.ces.iisc.ernet.in/energy/water/paper/wetland/study.html

RTO (Regional Transport Office). (2018). Annual report of the transport department of Karnataka compiled from RTOs. www.rto.kar.nic.in

Sedgwick, P. (2014). Relative risk versus odds ratio. *British Medical Journal*, *348*, 1407–1422.

Srinivasan, K. K., Gautam, N., Pradhan, G., & Naidu, G. M. (2007). Commute mode choice in a developing country: Role of subjective factors and variations in responsiveness across captive, semi captive and choice segments. *Transportation Research Record: Journal of Transportation Research Record*, *1*, 53–61. https://doi.org/10.3141/2038-07

Steg, L., Geurs, K., & Ras, M. (2001). The effects of motivational factors on car use: A multidisciplinary modeling approach. *Transportation Research A*, *35*, 789–806.

TERI (The Energy and Resource Institute). (2015). Energy data yearbook and directory 2016–14. TERI.

ThamizhArasan, V., & Vedagiri, P. (2011). Modeling modal shift from personal vehicle to bus on introduction of bus priority measures. *Asian Transport Studies*, *1*(3), 288–302.

Thompson-Graves, S., DuRoss, M., Ratledge, C. E., & Racca, P. D. (2006). Developing a state-wide travel demand model from a person based time series household survey. *Transportation Research Record*, *1*, 68–75.

TomTom. (2020). TomTom congestion index. TomTom International. www.tomtom.com

Transport Karnataka. (2001–2018). Vehicle registration data, Karnataka Transport Department. www.transport.karnataka.gov.in

Tyrinopoulos, Y., & Antoniou, C. (2013). Factors affecting modal choice in urban mobility. *European Transport Research Review*, *5*, 27–29.

von Thünen, J. H. (1826). *The isolated state*, translated into English (1966). Pergamon Press.

Chapter 4

Economic Cost of Traffic Congestion in Bengaluru

4.1 Introduction

We know that Bengaluru suffers from severe form of traffic congestion. Now it is high time to quantify its ill effects to internalize them. The prolonged delays tend to impose a huge economic loss in the form of opportunity cost and loss of productivity. Research studies by Wallis and Lupton (2013) for Auckland, Infra/IWW (2000) for Western Europe, Newbery (1999) for the UK, Scottish Executive (2005) for Scotland, ECMT (2003) for the UK, Transport Canada (2006) for urban areas of Canada have attempted to capture these economic losses. This has helped them to internalize the negative externalities of traffic congestion effectively and attain sustainable mobility. This highlights that a proper quantification effort would throw light on the economic consequences of the problem and help in formulating better policy measures. Otherwise, policy measures to handle the traffic flow will be lopsided. For instance, among the limited Indian studies which attempted to quantify the traffic congestion costs, most of them have based their estimates on the traditional engineering approach of speed-flow techniques. Often such measures indicate the inadequacy of the road infrastructure and offered the policy to implement supply-side policy measures. Economists have proved that such measures are ineffective and costly to the economy due to the operation of Braess Paradox (2005)[1].

The same holds true for Bengaluru city. Even in recent studies (BCG, 2018; TomTom, 2020), the attempt to quantify the traffic congestion costs considered only the travel time index[2] rather than the traffic time. The travel time index advocates the free-flow speed, which is economically not a viable measure. Instead, there is a need to quantify the external costs of congestion by considering the optimal speed and determining the optimal travel. This requires an economic approach to quantification. Such an approach will shift the policy's dimension from short- period measures to a more sustainable way of handling the traffic flow. Hence, this chapter provides estimations of economic costs of traffic congestion by providing details on the methodology adopted for each type of cost.

DOI: 10.4324/9781032662299-4

4.2 Methodology and Estimates of Economic Cost of Traffic Congestion

As we adopt the economic approach to quantify the traffic congestion costs, this approach defines the congestion costs as the additional costs on the road users who are not only the victims but are also the cause of the problem. The optimal speed of travel is taken as 40–50 kmph (adopted from DULT, 2011), rather than free-flow speed to compare the congested travel. The economic costs of traffic congestion are classified into direct and indirect costs. *Direct costs* are the costs borne by the drivers on the traffic stream, and *indirect costs* are the costs which are imposed on other non-drivers on the road.

4.2.1 *Direct Economic Costs of Traffic Congestion*

Under the direct cost category, the study has identified two important costs viz., time delay cost (TDC) and fuel wastage cost (FWC). Each of these costs is borne by the commuters who travel in their vehicle.

4.2.1.1 Time Delay Costs (TDC)

This cost is defined as the cost borne by drivers due to the loss of opportunity cost of time by travelling in a congested network. A prominent aspect of time delay cost is the value of traffic time (VOTT). VOTT differs from the value of travel time. It considers the time stuck in traffic as the additional time taken in the travel activity. Generally, this cost goes unaccounted for, as the commuters ignore that the time stuck in traffic has an opportunity cost. As the time stuck in traffic is generally dead-weight loss indicating an economic loss, we attach a monetary value to it. This is to be based on classical theoretical underpinning on value of traffic time.

4.2.1.2 Theoretical Background for the Value of Traffic Time

Understanding the value of traffic time will trace its roots in the classical theory of time allocation. The fundamental economic theory of time allocation behaviour dates back to the pioneering works of Becker (1965), Evans (1972) and DeSerpa (1971). DeSerpa (1971) identified the disutility associated with the impediment in travelling. Though there is a universal agreement that the value of travel time is an essential element of transport planning, there is a considerable argument in the method of valuation. Owing to complexities and subjectivities involved in stated preference approach, the study has adopted the revealed preference approach of the wage-rate model as formulated by Oort (1969), Johnson (1964), Train and McFadden (1978), and Forsyth (1980).

Conceptually, the welfare loss due to an increase in traffic time can be derived from the sum of money values which individuals attach to their time savings (Oort, 1969). It is assumed that the increase in traffic time is equivalent to the decrease in productive time to work or leisure to the individual.

According to traditional economic theory, the value of travel is presumed to be equivalent to the wage rate based on utility (welfare) function:

$$U = U\,(G, L) \ldots \tag{4.1}$$

$$\text{s.t.: } G + C_m = {}_wT_w \ldots \tag{4.2}$$

$$L + T_w + t_m = T \ldots \tag{4.3}$$

In which G and L are consumption of goods and leisure time, respectively. C_m is travel cost and t_m is travel time spent in mode m. T_w is working hours, w is the wage rate, and T is the total time available. Substituting Equation (4.3) in Equation (4.2) for T_w to derive the aggregate constraint as: $G + C_m - {}_wT + {}_wt_m + {}_wL$.

The Lagrangean used for solving the problem will be

$$Z = u\,(G, L) + \lambda\,(G + C_m - {}_wT + {}_wt_m + {}_wL) \ldots \tag{4.4}$$

The first-order condition for maximum utility with respect to goods is $\partial U/\partial G = \lambda$ and with respect to leisure time will be $\partial U/\partial L = \lambda w$. The value of travel time reduction (value of traffic time) can be derived as (adopted from Jara-Diaz & Farah, 1987; and Train & McFadden, 1978):

$$VOTT = \frac{\partial U / \partial L}{\partial U / \partial G} = w \tag{4.5}$$

Based on the theoretical explanation provided in the works of Jara-Diaz and Farah (1987) and Train and McFadden (1978), it is assumed that the time stuck in traffic is the productive time loss to which income of the individual can be attached. Equation (4.5) shows the value of travel time reduction (value of traffic time) is equal to the value of leisure time and both equal to wage rate (Shiaw, 1997). This indicates that an increase in travel time will reduce the leisure time of the individuals whose value can be derived from their wages. Many studies have indicated that the value of travel time is positively linked to income levels (Waters II, 1994; Forsyth, 1980). O'dea (1994) proved that the value of travel time savings (or increase) would be equal to the wage rate. Pearman and Button (1984), on the other hand, have classified the value of time into work time and non-work time. In the case of work time, the value is derived from conventional marginal productivity theory and hence is equal to wage. On the contrary, the value of non-work time has its theoretical basis in marginal utility theory, and it should be equal to wage rate as workers trade off leisure against work.

Following this framework, we have considered the hourly wages of commuters by taking their monthly income and adjusting for a number of hours of work in a day and number of workdays in a month. Though it is widely argued that the wage rate cannot be well a representative of the value of travel time, it has served as an important basis for the estimation of congestion costs in many studies. Prominent studies like Glanville and Smeed (1958), TTI (2012), DfT (2004), and Canada Transport (2006) have estimated the costs of road congestion using the average hourly wage of commuters.

The methodology used to derive time delay cost would be formulated as:

$$TDC = TT \times VOTT$$

Where TDC is time delay cost, TT is time lost in traffic (in hours), and VOTT is the value of traffic time.

4.2.1.3 Time Delay Cost on Private Vehicle Users

The time lost in traffic is considered as additional time[3]being lost in each junction by the drivers to which the value of traffic time (hourly wage rate) is attached. We have estimated the TDC separately for private vehicles and public vehicles. The private vehicles' TDC forms the direct cost, the public vehicles' TDC is taken as indirect cost (the cost imposed on them by private vehicles).[4]

Using the primary data, it is estimated that on average, a private vehicle user is stuck in traffic for 38 minutes a day. Considering the average working hour (8 hours/day) and average working days in a month (5.6 days/month), the average delay time for a year can be estimated as 168 hours/year per person which accounts for 7.3 days in a year.

A private vehicle user in the city loses Rs. 229 for every hour stuck in traffic and on average he/she may have to bear Rs. 40, 661 per year (Table 4.1). This cost accounts for almost 9.69 per cent of the per capita income of the respondents. The total annual time delay cost borne by private vehicle users in the sample is Rs. 1.10 crores. Table 4.1 also indicates that among the four zones, the annual time delay cost of Zone 1 and 4 is comparatively high. The CBD is choked with density of economic activity, whereas the peripheral zone (Zone 4) struggles to handle the interdistrict and state traffic. In terms of different private vehicles, the estimates reveal that, a two-wheeler user will bear Rs. 181 for every hour due to traffic congestion, whereas car users would bear a much higher cost of Rs. 380/hour. This does not indicate that the two-wheelers are the better mode of transportation in the city. Due to the higher occupancy rate, cars tend to wait a longer time than the two-wheelers and hence bear high cost.

Table 4.1 Zonal-wise annual time delay cost estimates for private vehicle users

Zone	*Annual TDC (Rs.)*	*Per capita TDC (Rs. / year)*	*TDC/hour (Rs./hour)*	*No. of delay hour in a year*	*No. days wasted in traffic in a year*
1	31,96,044	45,658	245	13,032	7.7
2	25,54,152	38,153	226	11,300	7
3	25,87,812	39,209	219	11,796	7.4
4	26,79,060	39,398	225	11,908	7.3
Total	**Rs. 1,10,17,068**	**Rs. 40,661**	**Rs. 229/ hour**	**48,036 hours**	**7.3 days**

Source: Authors' analysis based on primary data.

4.2.1.4 Fuel Wastage Cost (FWC)

FWC is referred to as the resource cost of traffic congestion which forms another significant direct cost borne by the drivers. When a vehicle traverses in congested traffic, it is not just time but fuel is also wasted. Studies like CRRI (2009) and Gangopadhaya and Parida (2008) have shown that vehicles consume more fuel when they stand in an idle condition or traverses less than fuel efficiency speed, as compared to the ideal speed of travel (40–50 kmph). Since this extra fuel consumed by vehicles due to traffic congestion is borne by the driver; the additional expenses on fuel are classified under the direct cost category. As there is a lack of studies which estimated the fuel wastage cost for Bengaluru our study makes an important contribution.

Methodology: The fuel consumed in traffic conditions needs careful consideration as it varies with different vehicles and type of engines. To adopt these technicalities of fuel usage by the vehicles, the methodology used by CSIR – CRRI (2009) and Gangopadhaya and Parida (2009) is adopted. The details of idle fuel consumption by vehicle type with their type of engines are provided in Appendix 4.1. The standard method for estimating the additional fuel cost as provided by IRC: 100 (1990) is:

Fuel wastage cost = Cost of fuel (Rs. /litre) x Fuel consumed in traffic situation (litres)

The cost of fuel is another important variable that depends on the price of fuel. As the price of fuel is highly volatile in nature, the average price (retail selling price) of the fuel in Bengaluru is taken for three months of the survey period (December 2018 to February 2019) from the Indian Oil Corporation.[5] The average price of petrol is taken as Rs. 74/litre and the average price of diesel as 67/litres.

4.2.1.5 Fuel Wastage Cost on Private Vehicle Users[6]

It is estimated by using the data on total hours of traffic delay; fuel consumed by each type of vehicle in idling condition and less than fuel efficiency speed condition multiplied by fuel price. The hours of traffic delay have been collected from the primary survey. As fuel consumption by vehicle depends on the type of vehicle, engine specification and speed of travel.[7] To account for these technicalities, the guidelines of CSIR – CRRI (2009) is followed. This report provides the guideline on fuel consumption in idle conditions by each type of vehicle. Further, the fuel efficiency speed depends on each type of vehicle. From the field investigation, it is found that the majority of vehicle's fuel efficiency speed is reported to be between 40 and 50 kmph, and this is also validated by DULT report on Bengaluru Mobility Indicator (2011).

In Table 4.2, aggregate fuel wastage cost from both two wheelers and cars are estimated. It can be stated that only from private vehicles around Rs. 45 lakhs worth of additional fuel is consumed (wasted) due to additional time stuck in traffic congestion.

Further, around 59,796 litres of additional fuel is consumed due to idling and slow movement of vehicles on the road. This indicates that every private vehicle commuter in the city has to bear an additional annual fuel expense of Rs. 16,618, which is almost 4 per cent of their PCI.

In terms of type of mode, it is estimated that car users bear an additional fuel cost of Rs. 32,182/year, whereas the two-wheeler users bear Rs. 11,461 every year. As our study is the first of its kind to make this estimation, we have provided an ideal travel cost estimated. This estimate will be our baseline estimate to compare the additional travel cost.

The ideal travel cost is defined as the normal cost of travel, borne by drivers when there are no additional traffic delays (they exit the signalized junction within one cycle) and they incur only fuel cost under optimal speed condition.[8] On the other hand, additional travel cost is the additional fuel cost borne by the drivers due to the traffic condition. Based on this, in the city, a private vehicle driver in the city is expected to bear an ideal travel cost of Rs. 17,335 per year. But his total travel is around Rs. 33,953 per year.

Table 4.2 Aggregate fuel wastage cost of private vehicle users

Zone	*FWC/year (in Rs.)*	*Per capita FWC (in Rs.)*	*Fuel wasted (ltrs)*
1	13,68,312	19,547	18,696
2	10,23,724	13,787	10,752
3	10,20,888	15,468	13,980
4	11,90,532	18,897	16,368
Total	**Rs. 45,03,456**	**Rs. 16,618**	**59,796 litres**

Source: Authors' analysis based on primary data.

The additional cost of Rs. 16,618 is the FWC borne by the commuters due to traffic congestion in the city. This is an imputed (hidden) cost of traffic congestion, and hence, called the external cost of traffic congestion in terms of resource wastage. If we compare this with the per capita income[9] of the respondents, instead of spending 4.13 per cent of income, commuters in the city are spending 8.09 per cent of their income on their travel. In this, commuters are not even aware of 5.96 per cent of their income is being spent additionally without any economic benefit.

4.2.1.6 Total Direct Economic Cost of Traffic Congestion

Summation of both time delay cost and fuel wastage cost borne by private vehicle users in the city gives the total direct economic cost of traffic congestion as:

$$TDEC = Time\ Delay\ Cost + Fuel\ Wastage\ Cost$$

or

$$TDEC = TDC + FWC$$

Table 4.3 provides the estimates of total direct economic cost for each zone. The city bears around Rs. 1.55 crores of the direct economic cost of congestion emerging from time delay and fuel wastages. That means, on average, a private vehicle user would bear a direct congestion cost of Rs. 57,271 every year.

Among all the zones, Zone 1's direct economic cost is showing much high number, which can be attributed to the busyness in the junctions. It is also proved in other estimates in the country like Chakrabartty and Gupta (2015) who estimated Rs. 2.66 crores as the congestion cost for CBD of Kolkata.

Table 4.3 Direct economic cost of traffic congestion for Bengaluru (in Rs.)

Zone	*TDC*	*FWC*	*Total TDEC*	*Per capita TDC*	*Per capita FWC*	*Per capita TDEC*
1	31,96,044	13,68,312	45,64,356	45,658	19,547	65,205
2	25,54,152	10,23,724	35,77,876	38,122	15,279	53,401
3	25,87,812	10,20,888	36,08,700	39,209	15,468	54,677
4	26,79,060	11,90,532	38,69,592	39,398	17,508	56,906
Total	**1,10,17,068**	**45,03,456**	**1,55,20,524**	**40,653**	**16,618**	**57,271**

Source: Authors' analysis based on primary data.

4.2.2 Indirect Economic Cost of Traffic Congestion

Indirect economic costs of traffic congestion are defined as the external costs as they are imposed on non-drivers like public transport user, pedestrians,[10] and society. In this category also, there are two major costs, namely, delay cost on non-drivers and health and productive cost. The health and productivity cost has been estimated separately in Chapter 5. Hence, in this section, the delay cost on non-drivers and productive hour loss is estimated.

Firstly, **the delay cost on non-drivers** is the time delay cost borne by other commuters who do not directly contribute to the congestion. For instance, public transport users bear an additional time cost due to the heavy traffic. The rationale for this treatment is, public transport is considered as a sustainable mode of transportation compared to private transport because of its high passenger-carrying capacity. Though the road space occupancy by public transport (bus) is higher than other vehicles (two wheeler or car), since its passenger occupancy (Buses = 50 passengers) is much higher than the private vehicles (two wheelers = 1; Cars = 4) it imposes a least cost on the economy. The methodology followed to estimate this cost is the same as the time delay cost under a direct cost category.

In Bengaluru city, there are two major public transport modes available for services: BMTC and Metro train. BMTC has a wide coverage of the routes in the city as compared to Metro trains (which is still in its infancy stage with two lines in operation by 2018). As the metro caters to only a few areas (in the study, it is operating in Zones 1 and 2), we found some commuters shifting from BMTC to Metro trains in these zones. Otherwise, BMTC is still act as dominant mode among public transport commuters of Bengaluru city. The estimates of TDC of non-drivers indicated in Table 4.4 reveal that public transport users in Zones 1 and 2 have less delay cost, which can be attributed to the meagre use of the mode and shifting from BMTC to metro trains. As Zones 3 and 4 are still to get the connectivity of the metro train,

Table 4.4 Zonal-wise annual time delay cost estimates for public vehicle users

Zone	*Annual TDC (Rs.)*	*Per capita TDC (Rs. /year)*	*TDC/hour (Rs.)*	*No. of hours delayed a year*	*No. of days stuck in traffic in a year*
1	8,54,136	23084.76	183	4,680	5.2
2	4,92,672	12632.62	100	4,968	5.2
3	9,64,332	22960.29	152	6,360	6
4	17,13,048	45080.21	250	6,840	7.5
Total	**Rs. 40,24,188**	**Rs. 25,796**	**Rs. 176/ hour**	**22,848 hours**	**6 days**

Source: Authors' analysis based on primary data.

hence face higher delay costs. This highlights the importance of public transport in reducing the costs.

A public vehicle user in the city bears an annual cost of Rs. 25,796 due to traffic congestion or it may cost Rs.176 per hour. The total cost of time delay for public mode user for the sample is around Rs. 40 lakhs per annum and almost 22,848 hours are lost in traffic congestion every year. This would account for almost six days in a year being stuck in traffic congestion.

Productive hour loss cost: Another unaccounted indirect cost of traffic congestion is the productivity loss. The productive hour loss cost is defined as the cost due to late arrival to workplaces due to traffic congestion. This is an implied cost borne by the economy which has a significant opportunity cost. Though there are many behavioural-oriented studies (Novaco et al., 1990; Hennessy & Wissenthal, 1999; Hennessy et al., 2000) that have examined the impact of commuting stress of workers on their productivity, our study differs in this respect. We estimated the costs borne by the workplaces due to the late arrivals of employees mainly due to traffic congestion. Hence, this study makes a novel contribution. The estimation of the value of traffic time for the productive hour is taken as the hourly wage of the respondents.

Often time delay estimates and a productive hour lost estimate are considered overlapping. To avoid such overlap, the data of only those respondents who reach their workplace late and do not extend their work hours are taken. From the primary survey, it is observed that some of the private companies would prefer their employees to have flexible hours. Still, when it comes to late arrival, they manage the productive hour lost by asking the employees to extend their work to cover the lost hour. But in sectors like government, banking and allied services, the work-hour extension is not considered either by employees or employers and neither have they reduced the wages of the employees. This will have a productivity impact on the economy, which is considered as frictional cost in the literature (Changik Jo, 2014).

For estimation, the productive hour is taken for the morning peak-hour congestion (from 8.30 AM to 10.30 AM[11]). In Table 4.5, out of 427 respondents, almost 34 per cent of the respondents reported that they arrive 5–10 minutes late to the workplace at least two days in a week and do not extend.

The total loss of a productive hour due to traffic congestion is 6,998 hours a year. This is leading to an annual loss of Rs. 11,45,568 to the economy. Among the four zones, productive hour loss is comparatively high in Zone 1 and Zone 4.

An interesting finding of this estimation is, though there is a general tendency among commuters to prefer private vehicle over public transport for the reason of it being the fastest mode, the estimation provides a contradictory finding. The respondents who use private vehicles often arrived late to the workplace than that of public transport users. This may be because public transport users tend to perceive the traffic congestion and travel time required for it and likewise makes their travel time arrangement.[12]

Table 4.5 Productive hour loss cost for Bengaluru

Zone	*No. hours lost (hours/year)*			*Annual cost (Rs.)*		
	Private vehicle users	*Public vehicle users*	*Hours lost total*	*Private vehicle users*	*Public vehicle users*	*Total*
1	1,632	554	2,186	2,65,668	1,20,264	3,85,932
2	1,188	576	1,764	1,39,104	66,816	2,05,920
3	1,072	516	1,588	138,444	87,792	2,26,236
4	1,428	432	1,860	2,00,640	1,26,840	3,27,480
Zonal Total	**4,920**	**2,078**		**Rs. 7,43,856**	**Rs. 4,01,712**	
Grand Total	**6,998 hours per year**			**Rs. 11,45,568**		

Source: Authors' analysis based on primary data.

4.2.3 *Total Indirect Economic Cost of Traffic Congestion*

This cost includes the time delay cost by the non-drivers (TDC (N)) and the productive hour loss cost (PHL). The total indirect cost of traffic congestion can be formulated as:

$$\text{TIEC} = \text{Time delay cost (by non-drivers)} + \text{Productive hour loss cost}$$

$$\text{TIEC} = \text{TDC (N)} + \text{PHL}$$

Table 4.6 provides the estimates of the total indirect economic cost of traffic congestion for each zone.

An annual cost of Rs. 40.24 lakhs in terms of time delay cost imposed on non-drivers and Rs. 11.45 lakh is the productive hour loss. This has accounted for around Rs. 51.69 lakhs of the annual indirect economic cost of traffic congestion. The per capita indirect economic cost for Zone 4 is

Table 4.6 Total indirect economic cost of traffic congestion (in Rs.)

Zones	*TDC (N)*	*PHL*	*TIEC*	*Per capita TDC (N)*	*Per capita PHL*	*Per capita TIEC*
1	8,54,136	3,85,932	1,240,068	23,084	6,225	29,309
2	4,92,672	2,05,920	6,98,592	12,632	3,677	16,309
3	9,64,332	2,26,236	11,90,568	22,960	2,977	25,937
4	17,13,048	3,27,480	20,40,528	45,080	6,421	51,501
Total	**40,24,188**	**11,45,568**	**69,759**	**25,796**	**4,676**	**30,472**

Source: Authors' analysis based on primary data.

Table 4.7 Annual total economic cost of traffic congestion (in Rs.)

Zone	*TDEC*	*TIDE*	*TEC*
1	45,64,356	12,40,068	58,04,424
2	35,77,876	6,98,592	42,76,468
3	36,08,700	11,90,568	47,99,268
4	38,69,592	20,40,528	59,10,120
Total	**Rs. 1,55,20,524**	**Rs. 51,69,756**	**Rs. 2,06,90,280**

Source: Authors' analysis based on primary data.

found to be high among all the zones. This can be attributed to lack of bus frequency and metro connectivity to the zone.

4.3 Total Economic Cost of Traffic Congestion

The total economic cost includes both direct and indirect costs of congestion for the city. It can be formulated as: ***Total Economic Cost = Direct Cost + Indirect Cost.*** That is, TEC = TDEC + TIDE[13]. The estimations are provided in Table 4.7:

The total economic cost of traffic congestion for the sample is estimated to be around Rs. 2.06 crores. An average commuter in the city bears an imputed cost of Rs. 48,455 (per person) a year which account for almost 11.55 per cent of their income. A total of 70,884 hours, which is, seven days in a year is being lost because of traffic congestion in Bengaluru. A private vehicle user would lose 7.3 days in a year and a public transport user is stuck for six days in a year in traffic congestion. Further, if a commuter is stuck for an hour in traffic, he/she would bear an average hourly cost of Rs. 212. If this cost is approximated to the working population of the city[14] (2017–2018), the total economic cost of traffic congestion would account to Rs. 245 billion, that is almost 0.58 per cent of the city's GDP.

4.4 Conclusion

Although the value of the reduction in travelling time is an important input to the infrastructure investment evaluation, it is often ignored that over-use of the facility would actually increase the travelling time indicating traffic congestion. This brings a negative impact on an individual's wellbeing. Hence, valuation of the traffic time should become an essential part of infrastructure evaluation. In this chapter, the negative impacts of traffic congestion are quantified in terms of direct and indirect cost for Bengaluru city. The total economic costs of traffic congestion account for Rs. 245 billion, which is almost 0.58 per cent of city's GDP (2017–2018). This clearly indicates the economic loss that urban planners are ignoring. Another key finding is among the four zones, due to lack of public transport, Zone 4 is incurring high indirect cost of congestion. This implies that city planners should divert their focus on improving the public transport system in the city.

Notes

1 Braess Paradox (2005) states that supply-side solution like adding new capacities to the road network will decrease the network performance and increase the travel time leading to further intensification of traffic congestion.
2 The index compared the congested speed to free-flow speed.
3 After considering the traffic signal cycle in each junction.
4 Public transport is sustainable mode of transportation and hence should be given prominence.
5 Largest commercial oil company in the country.
6 Estimates for public transport like bus is not considered by the study as it involves certain technical complexities in estimation.
7 There are other factors like road roughness and condition of the road which affects the fuel consumption by a vehicle is taken as per the specification provided by IRC.
8 The optimal speed is taken as 40–50 kmph for Bengaluru city.
9 The sample per capita income is Rs. 4,19,424.
10 The share of non-motorized transport users is less than 1 per cent and unable to account here.
11 Observations from field survey.
12 As observed from the field survey.
13 TDC and productive hour lost will include both private vehicle user cost and public vehicle user cost.
14 As the quantification is conducted for the working commuters, the estimates is approximated to working population of the city rather than the total population.

References

BCG (Boston Consulting Group). (2018). Unlocking cities: The impact of ridesharing across India, reported by Chin V, Mariam Jaafar, Suresh Subudhi. Nikita Shelomentsev, Duong Do and Irfan Prawiradinata, commissioned by UBER. www.bcg.com

Becker, G. S. (1965). A theory of the allocation of time. *Economic Journal*, *75*, 493–517.

Braess, D., Nagurney, A., & Wakolbinger, T. (2005). On a paradox of traffic planning. *Transportation Science*, *39*(4), 446–450.

Chakrabartty, A., & Gupta, S. (2015). Estimation of congestion cost in the city of Kolkata-A case study. *Current Urban Studies*, *3*, 95–104. https://doi.org/10.4236/cus.2015.32009

CRRI Report. (2009). Study on losses of petroleum products at traffic intersections due to idling of vehicles at Delhi, Centre for Road. Research Institute.

DeSerpa, A. C. (1971). A theory of the economics of time. *The Economic Journal*, *81*(324), 828–846.

ECMT (European Conference of Ministers of Transport). (2003). *Reforming transport taxes and charges*. OECD Publications Services. www.oecd-ilibrary.org

Dft (Department for Transport). (2004). Feasibility study of road pricing in the UK. Department for Transport.

DULT (Directorate of Urban Land Transport). (2008 & 2011). Bangalore urban mobility indicators 2008 and 2010–11. Draft final report, by Urban Mass Transit Company Limited.

Evans, A. (1972). On the theory of the valuation and allocation of time. *Scottish Journal of Political Economy*, *19*(1), 1–17.

Forsyth, P. J. (1980). The value of time in an economy with taxation. *Journal of Transport Economics and Policy*, *14*(3), 337–362.

Gangopadhaya, S., & Parida, P. (2008). Estimation of fuel loss during idling of vehicles at signalized intersection in Delhi. *Journal of Indian Road Congress*, paper no. 539.

Glanville, W. H., & Smeed, R. J. (1958). The basic requirement for the roads of Great Britain. *Proceedings of conference on the highway needs of Great Britain*. Institution of Civil Engineers.

Hennessy, D. A., & Wiesenthal, D. L. (1999). Traffic congestion stress and driver aggression. *Aggressive Behaviour*, *25*(6), 409–423.

Hennessy, D. A., Wiesenthal, D. L., & Kohn, P. M. (2000). The influence of traffic congestion, daily hassles and trait stress susceptibility on state driver stress: An interactive perspective. *Journal of Applied Biobehavioural Research*, *5*(2), 162–179.

Infra/IWW. (2000). External cost of Transport, accident, environmental and congestion cost in Western Europe. www.cedelft.eu

IRC:100 (Indian Road Congress). (1990). Guidelines for capacity of urban roads in plain areas. IRC.

Jara-Diaz, S. R., & Farah, M. (1987). Transport demand and users' benefits with fixed income: The goods/leisure trade-off revisited. *Transportation Research*, *21B*, 165–170.

Jo, C. (2014). Cost of illness: Concepts, scopes and methods. *Clinical and Molecular Hepatology*. https://doi.org/10.3350/cmh2014.20.4.327

Johnson, B. M. (1964). On the economics of road congestion. *Econometrica*, *32*(1/2), 137–150.

Novaco, W. R., Stokols, D., & Milanesi, L. (1990). Objective and subjective dimensions of travel impedance as determinant of commuting stress. *American Journal of Community Psychology*, *18*(2), 231–257.

O'dea, W. P. (1994). The value of travel time saving to an individual. *International Journal of Transport Economics*, *21*(3), 255–267.

Oort, C. J. (1969). The evaluation of travelling time. *Journal of Transport Economics and Policy*, *3*(3), 279–286.

Pearman, A. D., & Button, K. J. (1984). The value of time in road investment appraisals in less developed countries. *International Journal of Transport Economics*, *11*(2/3), 135–148.

Scottish Executive. (2005). Congestion on Scottish trunk roads 2003. Scottish Executive.

Shiaw, M. (1997). Value of leisure time based on individual mode choice behavior. *Journal of Advanced Transportation*, *38*(2), 147–168.

Train, K., & McFadden, D. (1978). The goods/leisure trade-off and disaggregate work trip mode choice models. *Transportation Research*, *12*, 349–353.

Texas Transportation Institute (TTI). (2012). Urban mobility report. http://mobility.tamu.edu/ums

TomTom. (2020). TomTom congestion index. TomTom International. www.tomtom.com

Transport Canada. (2006). The cost of urban congestion in Canada. Transport Department.

Waters II, A. G. (1994). The value of travel time savings and the link with income: Implications for public project evaluation. *International Journal of Transport Economics*, *21*(3), 243–253.

Wallis, I., & Lupton, D. (2013). The costs of congestion reappraised. NZ Transport Agency research report. 489. 65.

Appendix 4.1: Idling fuel consumption (ml/hour)

Vehicle Type	*Fuel consumed (ml/hr)*	*Type of Fuel*
Pulser	166	Petrol (4-Stroke)
Honda Active	118	Petrol
Maruti Van	692	Petrol
Mahindra Jeep	1052	Diesel
Tata Sumo	717	Diesel (Turbo Engine)
Tata Indica	547	Diesel
Esteem	740	MPFI
Hyundai Santro	563	Petrol
Taxi	1010	CNG
Bus	3610	CNG
Light commercial vehicles	690	Diesel
Heavy commercial vehicles	920	Diesel
Auto	700	CNG

Source: Gangopadhyaya and Parida (2008) and CRRI (2009)

Chapter 5

Health and Productivity Cost of Traffic Congestion

5.1 Introduction

We have discussed the economic cost of traffic congestion in the previous chapter. In terms of externality, though time and fuel cost are significant, another important implicit cost is observed on the health of environment and society. Vehicular pollution is proved to have an grievous impact on human health. Especially, when there is slow movement of vehicles, it will have a high concentration of pollutants. The World Health Organization (WHO) (2015) reported that nearly half of the air pollution in urban world is caused by vehicular emission. Even in case of India, nearly 72 per cent of the total urban air pollution is caused by vehicular emissions in Indian cities (TERI, 2015).[1] In a report by Health Effect Institute (HEI) (2019) found that among the top ten developing countries, India ranks second in position (next to China) with the highest mortality attributable to air pollution. Organization for Economic Co-operation and Development (OECD) (2014) estimated that 12 per cent increase in the number of deaths and 3 per cent decrease in years of life due to vehicular emission. This resulted in a death toll of around US$ 4.16 million in the year 2010. Another study by HEI (2010) estimated that approximately 1.2 million premature deaths in 2017 are caused by air pollution in India and more than half of it can be attributed to road transport-related pollution.

Even though research studies have examined the impact of air pollution on the environment, they do not account for source-specific impact. The source-specific apportionment would help to frame specific policy actions. One method of apportioning the impact of a source-specific air pollutant is to observe its effects on the health of society. Generally, source-apportionments studies consider major sources of air pollution like industries or sector-wise sources. But efforts to account for activity-specific sources like traffic congestion are very rare in the literature. In this line, our study makes a novel effort.

Hence, this chapter delves deep into the health and productivity impacts of traffic congestion. For this, we have given both epidemiological evidence and econometric analysis support for the city. Using scientific methods, we

DOI: 10.4324/9781032662299-5

accounted for both morbidity and mortality impacts of vehicular emissions. Our study begins by providing a background for the relation between traffic-related air pollutant and its impact on health.

5.2 Relation between Traffic-Related Air Pollutants and Its Health Impacts

We examined the source-specific pollutants (related to traffic congestion) and analyzed the intensity of the pollution concentration in the traffic junctions. For this, we made three main assumptions: (a) in traffic congestion, the level of vehicular emissions gets concentrated due to high vehicular density; (b) in high traffic density places, the impact of pollutants on human health is severe, and (c) due to regular travel, employed commuters are constantly exposed to a high level of emissions and hence face high health risks. To prove these hypotheses, we relied on both epidemiological and statistical evidence provided in the literature.

Epidemiological evidence analyzes the impact of each pollutant on human health. Vehicular pollutants are classified into primary pollutants and secondary pollutants. Primary pollutants are the one which gets generated at source and then dispersed. In the case of vehicular pollutants, primary pollutants are CO_2, CO, hydrocarbon (HC), particulate matters (PM), No_x, and substances called mobile source air toxins like benzene, formaldehyde, acetaldehyde, and 1,3-butadiene. Secondary pollutants are formed due to chemical interactions with air (Auto Fuel Policy, 2014). For example, oxidation of NO turns into NO_2 and ozone (O_3). These will have significant spatial effects. In case of traffic pollutants, the highest direct exposures are likely to occur at a local scale, i.e., mainly in traffic junctions. It is measured that, the average concentration of $PM_{2.5}$ in-vehicle is 2.5 times higher, and CO is 6 times higher than concentration nearby urban site (Chan et al., 1991; Adams et al., 2001; Kaur et al., 2005). Figure 5.1 provides a graphical representation of the chemical transformation of vehicular emission.

The early stage of exhaust contains CO_2, H_2O, CO, NO, NO_2, HC, semi-volatile organic compounds, inorganic materials, and PM from the exit of tailpipes at relatively high temperatures and concentration. This exhaust plume will mix with (entrain) background air, and there is a possibility of chemical diffusion-limited reaction taking place. This phenomenon is very localized and likely to affect exposure within 100 metres of the source. It means commuters in the traffic junctions have high exposure to these pollutants. At a greater distance, traffic emissions are more likely to get mixed up with other sources and are difficult to apportion.

Even among vehicular pollutants, there are two sources, viz., combustion and non-combustion source. The combustion sources are carbon monoxide, nitrogen oxide, and PM, which are emitted due to fuel usage and hence called tail-pipe emissions. Non-combustion sources are trace metals and organics

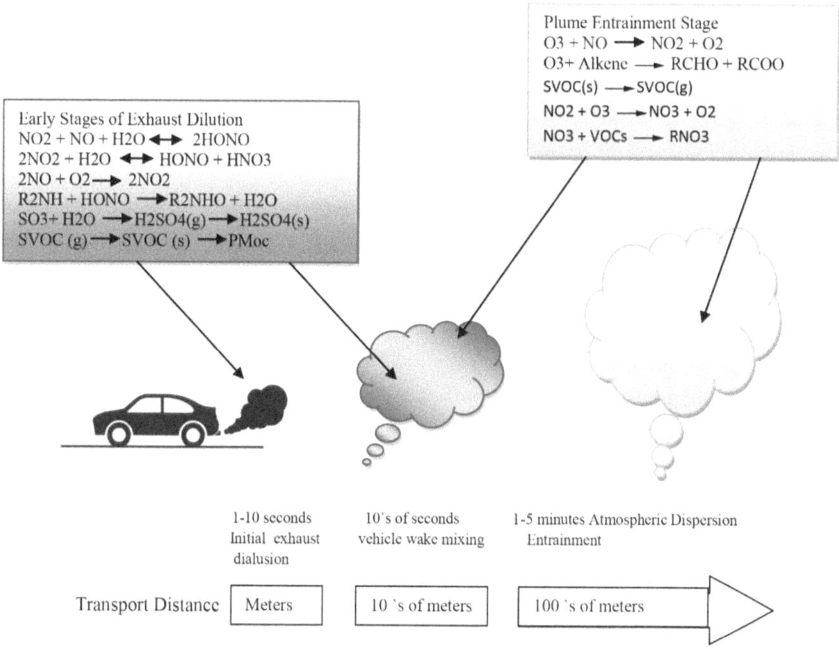

Figure 5.1 Schematic Representation of the Possible Chemical Transformation of Vehicle Emissions.

Source: Adopted from HEI, 2010.

that are emitted from travel movement of vehicles on the road (friction of tire on the road) (HEI, 2010). Among these two sources, the non-combustion source is difficult to trace and even the emission-monitoring data do not have such classification. Further, combustion emissions from vehicles account for up to 30 per cent of fine PM (less than 2.5 μm in aerodynamic diameter or $PM_{2.5}$) (WHO, 2005). Hence, only the combustion source and mainly the impact of $PM_{2.5}$ on the health of commuters in the city are analyzed. Before we proceed to the city level, this impact will be provided with epidemiological evidence.

5.2.1 *Health Effects of Traffic-Related Air Pollutants: Epidemiological[2] Evidence*

Notable studies have proved that criteria pollutants[3] have an adverse effect on human health (Pervin et al., 2008). Motor vehicle emissions have a variety of effects on human health which vary from itchy eyes to chronic lung disease or heart failure (McCubbin & Delucchi, 1999). WHO (2013)

Table 5.1 Traffic-related pollutants and possible health impacts

Pollutants	*Short-term impact*	*Long-term impact*	*Sources*
Fine particulates $PM_{2.5}$ and PM_{10}	Hospital admission for respiratory disease; asthma; exacerbated lung and heart condition	Premature death; affects the quality of life	COMEAP, 2009; AQEG, 2012
Ozone (O_3)	Respiratory irritation, asthma	Cardiovascular disease through prolonged inflammatory effects on lungs; myocardial infarction; and cardiac arrhythmias in older people	WHO, 2005; Schwartz &Zeger, 1990; McCubbin & Delucchi, 1999
Nitrogen dioxide (NO_2)	Bronchoconstriction, increased bronchial reactivity, airway inflammation	Decreased pulmonary function, inflammation of the lung and immunological changes	COMEAP, 2011; HEI,2010

reported that increased PM pollution created a substantial burden of disease which can take the form of loss of productivity, morbidity, and even mortality impacts.

There are many studies which have proved the instances of mortality and morbidity related to exposure to traffic-related air pollution. For instance, studies by Stern et al. (1988) and Balarajan and McDowall (1988) found high cases of mortality among bus drivers. Schwartz et al. (2002) and Jerrett et al. (2005) showed a relationship between mortality and increase in $PM_{2.5}$.

With respect to morbidity, HEI (2010) report indicated an association between cardiovascular morbidity, asthma and breathing problem, and lung issues with long exposure to traffic-related air pollution. Even in India, similar results are found (Dewaram et al., 1997; TERI, 2015; Balashanmugam et al., 2015). In this backdrop, we will proceed to analyze the impacts of traffic-related air pollutant in the city. For this, we have built the analytical framework and discussed the suitable methodology in the next section.

5.3 Analytical Framework and Methodology for Health Cost Estimation

WHO's environmental health criteria for assessing human exposure define transport air pollution exposure to include the concentration of pollutants in µg/m³ or any other equally valid metric; duration of exposure; and settings like the workplace, transport mode, and exposed population (WHO,

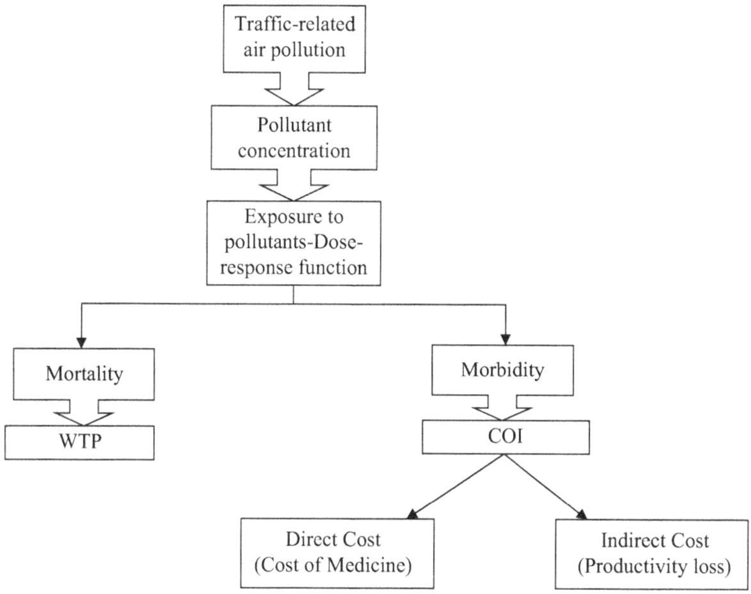

Figure 5.2 Empirical Framework of Estimation of Traffic-Related Health Cost.

Source: Author.

2005). Based on this definition and the kind of pollutant diffusion impact, we considered that in general, traffic junctions have elevated pollutant's concentration, and commuters stuck in these junctions tend to have a high exposure to pollution and are more prone to the health risks. From the epidemiological evidence, $PM_{2.5}$ has been identified as the most critical and primary pollutant from automobile emission.[4] The daily commuters are taken as per the definition of WHO (2005) who are exposed to high levels of $PM_{2.5}$ due to traffic congestion and are assumed to be more prone to serious health issues.

The health impacts of traffic-induced air pollution are divided into morbidity (or sickness) and mortality (premature deaths). Figure 5.2 will provide the analytical framework for the estimation of health impacts and the valuation techniques used in the study.

For estimating the health cost, it is important to establish the dose-response function (DRF). The DRF will establish the possible relation between the criteria pollutant and its health impact. Generally, either medical experiments or epidemiological evidence are required to establish this relationship. As medical experiments are not the scope of this study, the DRF is derived from the latter method. This is also supported by scientific econometric analysis.

The establishment of DRF should begin with understanding the health profile of the commuters. The proceeding section provides the details.

5.4 Health Profile of Study Area

The health profile describes the health issues faced by the commuters due to prolonged traffic delays and exposure to pollutants. Among 427 interviews, almost 73.5 per cent of the commuters reported that they suffer from traffic-related health issues due to long travels for work[5] and prolonged delays due to traffic congestion. The cases of stress and headache are very common (39%).[6] Issues like respiratory infections (27.3%) and asthma (20.3%) are considered chronic diseases due to vehicular emissions, mainly $PM_{2.5}$ (Parikh, 2004). 22.6 per cent of the respondents reported that they suffer from back pain due to long delays. A small section of respondents (18.4%) attributed the issue of skin allergy to vehicular pollution.

One major factor influencing the health status of respondents is age. It is common that traffic-related health issues get aggravated with age. Around 22.5 per cent of the respondents who belong to the age group of less than 25 years reported that they suffer from after-travel headaches and stress. About 17.5 per cent reported that they have skin allergies due to traffic emissions. But among the age group above 35 years, the most commonly reported travel-related health issues are respiratory infection, back pain, and headache. Figure 5.3 provides details about the age-wise health issue reported by the respondents in the study area.[7]

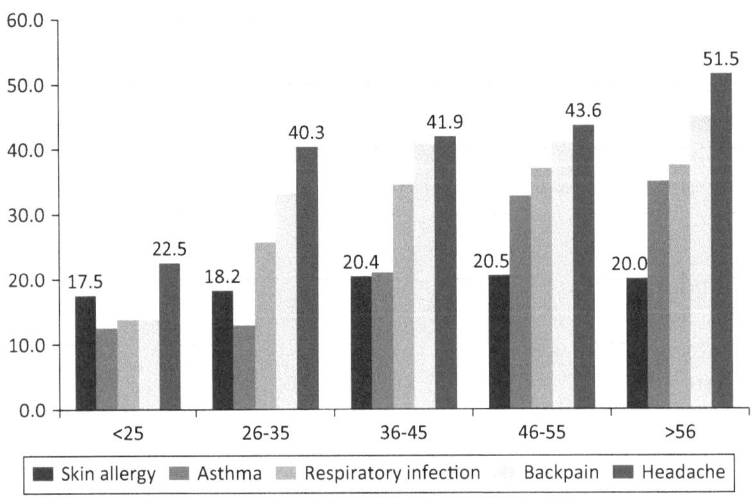

Figure 5.3 Age-wise Travel-Related Health Issues Suffered.

Source: Authors' analysis based on primary data

Table 5.2 Average traffic exposure and distance travelled by disease type classification

Details	*Asthma*	*Stress and headache*	*Respiratory infection*	*Back pain*	*Skin allergy*
Average distance travelled (kms/day)	34.5	22.5	35.2	32.25	28.4
Average traffic exposure (min/day)	43.5	30.4	42.7	32.7	29.2

Source: Authors' analysis based on primary data.

For traffic-related impacts, the travel length and exposure are key variables. Even epidemiological evidence proved that prolonged exposure to traffic emission would result in high cases of chronic illnesses like respiratory infection and asthma among the commuters.

This argument holds true even for the city. We found that, if a commuter travel more than 34 kms a day and is exposed to 43.5 minutes/day of traffic emissions, he/she is more likely to suffer from the issue of asthma. Similarly, 35 kms of travel and 42.7 minutes of exposure may lead to respiratory infections among the commuters in the city.

5.5 Economic Valuation of Health Cost: Morbidity and Mortality

5.5.1 Morbidity Impacts: The Dose–Response Relationship

The dose–response function (DRF) for morbidity impacts is established by considering the daily commuter's travel and health details. The $PM_{2.5}$ effect on them is observed by collecting its data from respective zones as provided by the Karnataka State Pollution Control Board (KSPCB). There are certain data associated problems like lack of historical data on the travel and health status and linkages to air pollution and its exposure. Further, while estimating the cost, people may not visit the hospital immediately for many traffic-induced health issues unless the issue becomes severe. To that extent, the result provides a lower limit of the economic cost of health due to traffic congestion.

To establish this DRF, we relied on econometric tools. As the data are based on the primary survey, the responses are not continuous but take discrete positions. To model this data, a logit model is used, which will provide the estimates of the probability of having an illness due to the impact of congestion-related variables. The logit specification is provided in Box 5.1.

Box 5.1 The Logit Model Specification

The dependent variable (y^*) is a latent variable and is not observable. Hence, we observe a qualitative variable y_i, defined by

$y_i = 1$ if $y_i > 0$

$= 0$ otherwise

$$y_i = \beta_0 + \sum_{j=1}^{k} \beta_j x_{ij} + u_i \quad (i)$$

1. Let P_i be the probability of $y_i = 1$; in our case, the subject is suffering from respiratory infection.
2. The error term is assumed to be logistic, and we obtain

$$y_i = \beta_0 + \sum_{j=1}^{k} \beta_j x_{ij} + u_i \quad (ii)$$

Then,

$$y_i = \beta_0 + \sum_{j=1}^{k} \beta_j x_{ij} + u_i \quad (iii)$$

The left-hand side of the equation (ii) is called a log-odds ratio. The log-odds ratio is a linear function of the explanatory variables. After estimating the parameter, we can predict the effect of changes of any of the explanatory variables on the probability of the observation belonging to either of the two groups (e.g., equation (iii)).

Source: Parikh, 2004, pg: 249.

The DRF in econometric form is written as:

$$\text{Resp} = \alpha_0 + \beta_1 \text{age} + \beta_2 \text{TTR} + \beta_3 \text{YTR\_2} + \beta_4 \text{YTR\_3} + \beta_5 \text{YTR\_4} + \beta_6 \text{TE} + \beta_7 \text{two\_wh} + \beta_8 \text{metro} + \beta_9 \ln \text{PM}_{2.5} + \mu \quad (5.1)$$

where α represents the constants and β represents coefficients of the variables, and μ is the error term. The descriptive statistics of the variables are provided in Table 5.3.

The logit function is interpreted as the probability function of suffering from the illness with respect to the change in the explanatory variables. The estimated probability equation for respiratory illness is provided in Table 5.4. The likelihood ratio (LR) Chi-square test confirms that at least one of the regression coefficients in the model is not equal to zero. The logit result

Table 5.3 Descriptive statistics with description of the variables used in the model

Variables	*Description*	*Mean*	*Std. dev*	*Min*	*Max*
Resp Yes-1 No-0	Respondents suffering from respiratory-related illness (dependent variable)	0.17	0.37	0	1
Age	Age of the respondents (in years)	33.96	9.44	18	72
TD	Time stuck in traffic congestion (in min/day)	38.81	18.98	0	130
Years of travel dummies[8]	Years of travel by the respondents	0.21	0.40	0	1
YTR_1(Base category)	Less than 4 years of travel	0.58	0.49	0	1
YTR_2	5–10 years	0.12	0.33	0	1
YTR_3	11–15 years	0.04	0.21	0	1
YTR_4	Above 16 years				
TTR	Total travel time is the time taken to reach the destination from the origin (in minutes)	8.43	5.33	1	40
Mode of vehicle dummies	Car users (base category)	0.15	0.36	0	1
Cars	Two-wheeler users	0.47	0.49	0	1
Two_wh	Metro users	0.36	0.48	0	1
Pub					
InPM2.5	log of $PM_{2.5}$ of each zone of the study area (in μgm^3)	4.58	0.20	4.26	4.78

indicates age, years of travel (YTR), time taken for daily travel (TTR), traffic delays (TD), and mode choice variables are statistically significant.

The result indicates that, as age increases, the probability of the respondents suffering from respiratory-related illness will also increase. In other words, a year increase in the age of the respondents will increase the respiratory illness by 0.5 per cent in the sample population. Even research studies cited in HEI (2010) report find similar results.

In the case of time taken to travel (TTR), the variable has a positive and significant impact on the dependent variable. In terms of the marginal effect, it can be described that one percent increase in the time taken to travel would increase the illness by 0.06 per cent. An interesting result was found in the case of years of travel (YTR) by the respondents, which is classified as four categories and introduced as dummy variables. The result indicates that the probability of respiratory-related illness increases with an increase in years of travel. From the marginal effect, it can be explained that the respondents who are travelling since more than 16 years are 6.6 per cent more likely to suffer from respiratory-related illness as compared to commuters travelling in the last four years (Base category). Similarly, with the case of respondents travelling for 5–10 years, the illness suffering may increase by 0.9 per cent

Table 5.4 Logit result for respiratory-related illness (traffic-related illness)

Dependent variable: resp (Yes = 1; No = 0)	*Logit model*		*Marginal effect*		*95% confidence interval*	
	Coefficient	*Std. error*	*dy/dx*	*Std. error*	*Lower*	*Upper*
Age	0.043[a]	0.015	0.005[a]	0.0019	0.0017	0.009
TTR	0.009[b]	0.004	0.001[b]	0.0006	7.86	0.002
YTR_2	0.744[b]	0.384	0.0091[b]	0.0044	0.0004	0.179
YTR_3	0.462	0.390	0.060	0.007	−0.086	0.219
YTR_4	0.418[a]	0.081	0.066[a]	0.040	−0.148	0.271
TD	0.012[b]	0.007	0.001[b]	0.0009	−0.002	0.003
Two_wh	0.741[b]	0.356	0.094[b]	0.045	−0.182	0.006
Metro	−0.450[a]	0.382	−0.055[a]	0.040	−1.44	0.033
lnPM2.5	0.198[b]	0.098	0.025[b]	0.007	−1.46	0.196
Constant	−5.17	3.32	–	–	–	–
LR $Chi^2(9)$	31.92[a]			hat – 1.19[a]		
Pseudo R^2	0.0811			hatsq – 0.07		
Hosmer & Lemeshow test (8)	6.04[a]			Constant – 0.09		

Source: Authors' calculation based on a primary survey.
[a]Significance at 1%; [b]significance at 5%; [c]significance at 10%.

as compared to respondents travelling since four years.[9] A plausible explanation is that commuters with long years of travel are more prone to the risk of traffic-related illness due to the constant and prolonged exposure of $PM_{2.5}$.

An important investigation that we have carried out is related to the impact of traffic delays. We found that the variable has a positive impact on respiratory-related illness by 0.1 per cent. This indicates the longer time of traffic would expose the commuters for a higher concentration of pollutants, and hence, may have a higher probability of respiratory-related illness. Similar results are found in CPCB (2011) and TERI (2015). A similar effect is found in the case of $PM_{2.5,}$ where the one unit increase in the pollutant may increase the respiratory-related illness cases by 2.5 per cent. This can also be interpreted as a 10 μgm^3 decrease in $PM_{2.5}$ from its current level would reduce the respiratory-related illness by 2.5 per cent in the zones.

In terms of modal impact, we found that two-wheeler users are 0.94 per cent more likely to suffer from the risk of respiratory-related illness as compared to car users. This can be linked to higher exposure to pollution to two-wheeler users than car users. An interesting result is found in the case of metro users in the city. As compared to private vehicle users, the metro users in the city are less likely to suffer from the respiratory-related illness caused by traffic congestion. This result highlights the importance of public transportation and its positive impact on health improvement. A similar result is found in the HEI (2010) report, which emphasizes that the improvement in public transport usage would significantly improve the health status among commuters.

In Table 5.4, the 95 per cent confidence interval column provides the upper and lower probability for the respective explanatory variable influence on the dependent variable. The model is tested for the goodness of fit using the Hosmer and Lemeshow's test (6.04) whose p-value is found insignificant, indicating the predicted frequency and observed frequency is matching closely and hence the model is fit. The specification error of the model is tested using 'linktest' command in Stata software. It is found that *hat* variable is significant at 1 per cent indicating the model is free from any specification error. The results are also free from multicollinearity as the standard errors are not inflated.

5.5.2 Economic Valuation of Morbidity due to Traffic Congestion

To measure the morbidity due to traffic-induced air pollution, the cost of illness approach is used. Under this method, two costs are considered viz., direct and indirect costs.[10] Under the direct cost of illness, a prominent out-of-pocket expenditure i.e., cost of medicines is taken, and under the indirect cost, the productivity loss has been estimated by taking the value of work-day loss (WDL) using the wage-rate method. The indirect cost also includes preventive expenditures which are the expenses made by commuters to avoid the congested route. Hence, the valuation of morbidity includes:

Cost of illness = direct cost (cost of medicines) + indirect cost (productivity loss and preventive expenses)

For direct cost of illness, we have taken the medical expenses as it forms prominent cost. It was found that out of 73.5 per cent of commuters who reported illness, nearly 67.19 per cent of them said they seek medical aid. The rest, 32.8 per cent respondents reported that even though they suffer from travel-related health issues, they avoid medical help as the issue gets subsided in a day or two. An important observation made from the data is that among this 32.8 per cent of respondents, the majority of them (78%) belong to the age below 30 years.

Among various traffic-related health issues, respiratory infection (30.5% of respondents), asthma (27.4), headache (20.7), back pain (10.2), and skill allergy (5.4) issues seek medical attention and hence bear an out-of-pocket expenditure (without any health insurance claims). Among the total 67.19 per cent of medical assistance seekers, nearly 27 per cent of the respondents incur cost ranging from Rs. 101–200 and around 23.2 per cent of them incur costs ranging from Rs. 401–600 (Figure 5.4).

In Table 5.5, details of medicine cost for the type of disease. The respiratory-related issues like asthma and respiratory infection incur the high cost of an average Rs. 690 and 354 per month, respectively.[11]

On average, a commuter in the city would spend around Rs. 412 per month as the cost of medicine due to the travel-related health issue. This would sum up to Rs. 4,944 per person per year spent as cost of illness. This

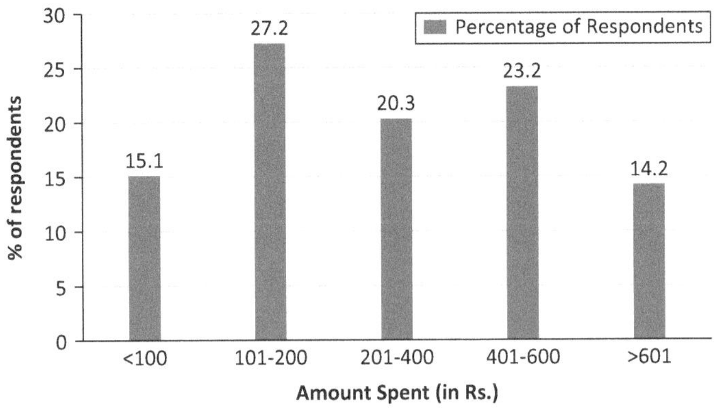

Figure 5.4 Percentage of Respondents Incurring the Cost of Medicine.

Source: Authors' Analysis Based on Primary Data.

Table 5.5 Cost incurred towards medicines

Diseases	*Average cost of medicine (Rs. PM)*
Asthma	690
Respiratory infection	354
Skin allergy	325
Back pain	286
Headache	222

Source: Primary data.

accounts for almost 1.17 per cent of the per capita income being spent as the out-of-pocket expenditure due to illness suffered due to traffic congestion.

5.5.2.1 Indirect Cost of Illness: Productivity Impacts

Apart from the out-of-pocket expenditures, illnesses impose certain implicit costs in the form of work absenteeism leading to productivity loss to the economy. It is measured as the cost of foregone earnings due to traffic-related illness, indicating an implied economic cost of traffic congestion.

The productivity impacts are estimated by collecting data of sick leave days from work due to traffic-related health issues. Utmost care has been taken while gathering the information on sick leave days from the respondents, as there might be other reasons for sick leave. To avoid the recall bias, the data are collected for the previous three months and cross verified with the employers wherever possible. Major issues for which sick leaves are taken are respiratory infection and asthma. The average days of sick leave taken by the respondents are nine days in a year. Other issues and sick leaves details are provided in Table 5.6.

Since the sick leaves will have productivity loss to the workplace, we considered it as economic loss due to traffic congestion. This loss is estimated using the average income of the sample. The annual productivity loss for the

Table 5.6 Details on productivity loss due to traffic-related health issues

Health issues	*% of respondents*	*Average days of sick leaves/year*
Respiratory infection	39.6	12
Asthma	32.8	12
Headache	15.7	08
Back pain	11.9	04

Source: Authors' analysis based on primary data.

traffic-related illness is estimated as Rs. 13,104 per person. This accounts for almost 3.12 per cent of the PCI being lost as the productivity impact of traffic congestion.

In health economic studies, there are certain preventive and mitigative measures. These measures are the steps taken to avoid the impact. For instance, people may prefer travelling on a less congested route or mode. In our case, Bengaluru has less congested route for some parts of the city. But this route has a toll (NICE road). In terms of mode, commuters may even prefer faster and safe modes like Metro. But these two measures do not cover the entire city. Hence, our estimate ignored these costs.

5.5.2.2 Economic Cost of Morbidity due to Traffic Congestion

The total cost of illness would sum up the direct and indirect cost of illness.

Cost of illness = Direct cost + Indirect cost

The cost of illness is estimated by adding up the annual average cost of medicine (direct cost) as Rs. 4,944 per person and an annual average loss of productivity (indirect cost)[12] as Rs. 13,104 per person. This would account for the total annual average cost of illness of Rs. 18,048 per person. Out of total annual personal income, direct cost accounts for 1.17 per cent and indirect cost accounts for 3.12 per cent. This clearly points out that commuters incur higher imputed (intangible) cost than the direct cost due to commuting in a congested route.

5.5.3 Mortality Impacts: The Dose–Response Relationship

The DRF for mortality is established using the key variables like population, PM, and vehicular growth. These variables are selected based on Parikh (2004) model. The attributable deaths due to traffic-induced air pollution are estimated from the total death rates in the city (2017–2018 data). Based on this, we formulated the equation as:

$$\text{TDR\%}_{\text{city}} = f(\text{lnpop}, \text{PM}_{2.5}, \text{lnvhcl}) \tag{5.2}$$

where TDR percent $_{\text{city}}$ = total death rate in the city, lnpop = log of city's population, $PM_{2.5}$ = average particulate matter 2.5 in µg/m^3, lnvhcl = log of registered vehicles in the city. The independent variables, $PM_{2.5}$ and vehicular population, are used to bring out their effect on the death rate of the city. The ordinary least square regression was conducted.

$$\underset{}{\text{TDR\%}_{\text{city}}} = \underset{(1.45)}{54.16} - \underset{(-1.35)}{4.80}\text{lnpop} + \underset{(1.04)}{2.12}\ \text{lnvhcl} + \underset{(0.10)}{0.00187}\text{pm2.5} \tag{5.3}$$

$R^2 = 53\%$

As expected, the total death rate increases with rising $PM_{2.5}$ levels. The coefficient of $PM_{2.5}$ and the vehicular population is significant at 5 per cent. The valuation exercise is to measure the change in the pollutants' concentration from its present level to the acceptable standard. For this, we have attempted to value the economic cost of a 10-unit change in $PM_{2.5}$ concentration from the present level. For this, a partial differential of the Equation (5.3) with respect to $PM_{2.5}$ is taken to get the excess death rate attributable to $PM_{2.5}$.

$$\frac{\partial TDR}{\partial \text{PM2.5}} = 0.00187$$

For a 10-unit change in $PM_{2.5}$, the number of attributable deaths can be calculated as:

Attributable death rate	= 0.00187 × 10
Normal death rate in Bengaluru	= 0.46% (NHSRC, 2018)
Population of Bengaluru (2018)	= 1,07,53,449
Number of normal deaths	= 0.46% * 1,07,53,449 = 49,446
Number of attributable deaths	= 0.018 * 49,466 = 910

This provides that 10-unit change in $PM_{2.5}$ in the city would lead to 910 numbers (0.018%) of attributable deaths.

5.5.4 *Economic Valuation of Mortality due to Traffic Congestion: Methodology*

Estimating the monetary value for the risk of mortality is often the most difficult part of health damage assessment (World Bank, 1997). This involves uncertainties in establishing the dose–response function (DRF). In this, assessing the economic cost of mortality from traffic-related air pollution is furthermore challenging. For established source-specific DRF, econometric tools are CVM methods are advocated to be appropriate (Lave & Seskin, 1970, 1973; Small, 1977). Based on this, we provided the DRF for mortality for Bengaluru. This is first of its kind study for an Indian city. For this, we elicited the willingness to pay for the reduction in traffic-related air pollution which will reduce the related mortality in the city.

The rationale for the selection of the CVM approach: The principle underlying Willingness To Pay is the belief that in market economies, the social cost of a change in economic outcomes is measured by the sum of individual's WTP for that change (World Bank, 1997). Appropriate valuation of premature mortality from air pollution is the amount that people are willing to pay for a marginal reduction in the risk of death from the cause. There are two methods to measure the WTP for reducing mortality risks:

compensating wage differential and contingent valuation. The compensating wage differential assumes, other things being equal, that workers in riskier jobs must be compensated with higher wages than workers in safer jobs. The differential in wages reflects what the individual is willing to give up if he moves to a safer job. Cropper et al. (1997) cautioned that studies which use compensating wage differential measured the compensation of mortality risk for the mid-year age group (around forty years). But death from traffic-related air pollution typically occurs at a later age than forty years, and therefore, this method would not provide a correct estimate. Further, in developing countries like India, wages do not give an accurate picture of the compensations.

The contingent valuation through the stated preferences method involves direct elicitation of WTP for reduced risk of mortality. Under this method, respondents are interviewed and provided with a hypothetical situation regarding the risk of mortality and probable measures. By delivering the payment vehicle for the measures, their willingness to pay for the measure will be elicited. This will be used for estimating the economic cost of mortality. In our WTP survey, we created a hypothetical situation. The respondents are informed that reduction in traffic-related emission would significantly improve the health condition (both morbidity and mortality). With this information, the respondents are probed to reveal their preference regarding State intervention with a policy to improve to reduce the vehicular pollution. The basis for their willingness (whether health expenses or income) is also taken into consideration.

The value of risk of mortality is derived by aggregating individual's WTP to secure a marginal reduction in the risk of premature death (OECD, 2014). The value captured here is the value of the reduction in the risk of dying to an individual and not the value of postponed revenue or the value of higher pension expenditure by the government (OECD, 2014).

5.5.5 *Economic Cost of Mortality due to Traffic Congestion*

Before estimating the cost of mortality, it is important to understand the factors affecting the willingness to pay for the reduction of risk of death from the traffic-related health issues.

5.5.5.1 Description of WTP for the Reduction of Air Pollution

Before examining the socio-economic variables, it is important to consider the zone-wise willingness to pay values (Table 5.7). This provides an analysis by relating the WTP values to zonal characteristics like the income level and air pollution quality of each zone. The average per capita income and average annual $PM_{2.5}$ are taken for the year 2018–2019.

Table 5.7 Zonal wise WTP values with their income and air pollution levels

Zones	*Average per capita income (Rs./year)*	*Average annual $PM_{2.5}$ level ($\mu g/m^3$)*	*WTP (% of respondents)*	
			Yes	*No*
1	5,05,368	70.9	90.6	9.3
2	5,21,100	120	92.4	7.5
3	5,02,716	95	85.1	14.8
4	4,37,176	113	63.2	36.7
All zones	4,19,424	87.91	82.9	17.1

Source: Authors' analysis based on primary data.

Table 5.8 Health issue-wise WTP

Health issues	*% of Respondents*	
	Yes	*No*
No disease	70.5	29.5
Asthma	91.3	8.6
Respiratory infections	92.8	7.14
Cough	88.8	11.11
BP and Stress	90.6	9.3
Headache	89	11

Source: Primary data.

Among the four zones, the WTP for the reduction in risk of death due to traffic-induced air pollution is high in Zones 1 and 2. This can be attributed to high vehicular density in these zones. Further, among different age groups, a maximum number of respondents belonging to the age group above forty-five years (90% of the age group) are willing to pay for the reduction in air pollution as compared to the age group below forty-five years. In terms of income, like other studies, we also found that WTP positively increases with the income. For instance, among the respondents of the income-class less than Rs. 10,000, only 28 per cent of them are willing to pay for the reduction of traffic-related air pollution. In contrast, in the case of the income group of above Rs. 55,000, all the respondents replied positively. Similar results are also found in the case of education.

It may be possible that the elicitation of values of WTP may depend on the health issue suffered by the respondents. But it is interesting to know that those commuters who do not suffer from any travel-related health issue (70.5%), still are willing to pay for the reduction in traffic-related air pollution. This infers that the respondents are aware of the probable impact of pollution and are willing to make contributions for the betterment.

Table 5.9 Description and descriptive statistics of variables used in the model

Variables	*Description*	*Mean*	*Std. dev*	*Min.*	*Max.*
WTP (Dependent variable)	Willingness to pay for a reduction in traffic-related emission: yes = 1; No = 0	0.82	0.37	0	1
Amount (dependent variable)	WTP amount (Rs./year)	376.5	397	0	3,000
Income	Annual income of commuters (in Rs.)	4,19,423	3,00,144	96,000	30,00,000
Gender	Sex of commuter: 1 = male; 0 = female	0.64	0.47	0	1
Age	Age of the respondents: Dummy variables are	0.18	0.39	0	1
	Dage1: Age below 25 years (reference category)	0.66	0.47	0	1
	Dage 2: Age between 26 and 45 years	0.14	0.35	0	1
	Dage 3: Age above 46 years				
Education	Education of the respondents: Dummy variables are	0.24	0.43	0	1
	Dedu 1: Education below graduation (reference category)	0.41	0.49	0	1
	Dedu 2: Graduation level	0.33	0.47	0	1
	Dedu 3: After graduation level				
Exposure	Time exposed (spent) in traffic emission (in minutes/day)	38.81	18.98	0	130
Treatment	Travel-related health issue treated	0.50	0.50	0	1
	yes = 1(if treatment is taken); no = 0				
WDL	Workdays loss due to travel-induced health issue	0.25	0.51	0	4
Awareness	Awareness regarding traffic-induced air pollution causing mortality risk	0.84	0.36	0	1
	1 = yes; 0 = otherwise				
Traffic_illness	Traffic-related illness suffering by the respondents	0.12	0.33	0	1
	1 = Yes; 0 = No				
Zones of the city	Z1 = Zone 1 = CBD (Reference category)	0.25	0.43	0	1
	Z2 = Zone 2 = Adjacent CBD	0.24	0.43	0	1
	Z3 = Zone 3 = Inner periphery	0.25	0.43	0	1
	Z4 = Zone 4 = Periphery	0.24	0.43	0	1

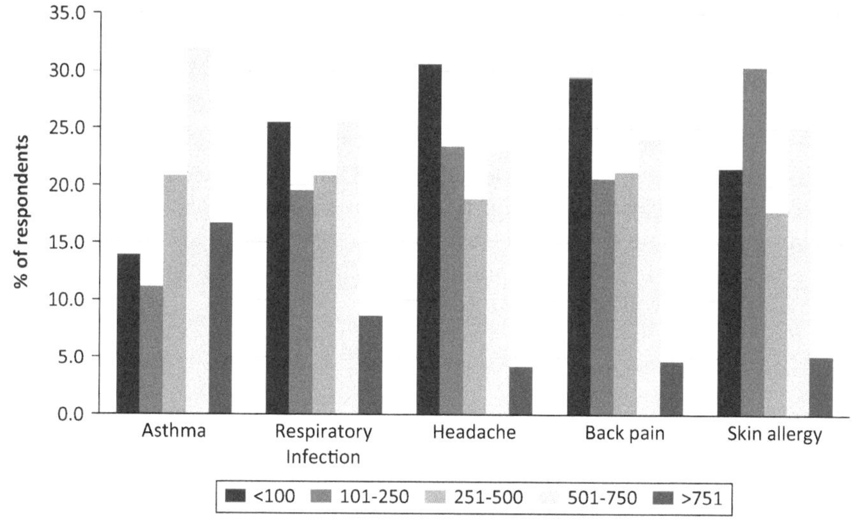

Figure 5.5 WTP Values Based on Disease Type.

Source: Authors' Analysis Based on Primary Data.

Further, among each disease type, a majority (above 80%) of the respondents are WTP for the reduction in traffic-related air pollution, which would reduce the related mortality.

Though we described the factors affecting WTP, in literature, there are scientific tools to verify the key factors and their impact. For this, we relied on the health production model.

It is assumed that the utility is derived from goods consumed X, leisure time L, workdays loss due to traffic-induced illness H, and level of air pollution Q. The individual derives utility from consumption of X and L and disutility from H and Q.

$$U = U(X, L, H, Q) \tag{5.5}$$

Further individual adopts certain mitigating activities which improve or maintain his health status given Q and other socio-economic characteristics Z. The health production function can be written as,

$$H = H(M, Q, Z) \tag{5.6}$$

The workdays loss H enters the budget constraint by influencing the amount of productive time available for work. Thus, the budget constraint can be formed as,

$$Y + w(T\text{-}L\text{-}H) = PxX + PmM \tag{5.7}$$

where Y is non-wage income, w is the wage rate, T is the total time available, and terms in parenthesis is time spent in working. P is the price of X and M. The health production model assumes that individual allocates time between work and leisure; and income between medicine and other goods to maximize the utility is subject to the budget constraint (Equation (5.7)).

An individual's willingness to pay the amount would be the amount that can be taken from him for reducing the vehicular emissions and keep his utility constant. This can be equivalent to the change in H. The value of change in H may be defined using a pseudo-expenditure function (Cropper & Freeman, 1991). This is the minimum value of expenditure minus wage income necessary to keep utility at U^0, or

$$E = \min \{PxX + PmM - w(T\text{-}L\text{-}H) + \lambda\,[U^0 - U(X, L, H, Q)]\} \tag{5.8}$$

where λ is a Lagrange multiplier. Willingness to pay for a non-marginal change in H may be defined as the expenditure necessary to achieve U^0 at the original workdays loss H^0, minus the expenditure necessary to achieve U^0 at the new (lower) workdays loss H^1

$$WTP = E(Px, Pm, Y, w, H^0, U^0) - E(Px, Pm, Y, w, H^1, U^0) \tag{5.9}$$

Equation (5.9) implies that willingness to pay should vary with income, prices of goods and medicines, individual characteristics, whether treatment is undertaken, and work-days loss. To validate the WTP responses, we regress it on these variables. In addition, WTP values are calculated based on mathematical expectations (discrete variables), and the formula is (Kong et al., 2014):

$$E = WTP = \sum_{i=1}^{n} \alpha_i Pr_i \tag{5.10}$$

Where α_i stands for the amount respondents *i* willing to pay, *Pri* is the probability that respondents will pay the amount; n is the sample size of the respondents whose WTP is positive.

5.5.5.2 *Factors influencing WTP and WTP amount*

For eliciting the WTP, we provided a hypothetical policy intervention. It explains that the WTP amount will reduce the morbidity and mortality impacts due to traffic congestion. To investigate the factors influencing willingness to pay for a reduction in traffic-related emissions, Heckman's two-step model is used. In this model, the first step uses the probit model to examine the factors affecting the willingness to pay and in the second step, the factors influencing the payment level using multiple linear regression model are used. The models can be expressed as:

$$Z = \partial_0 + \partial_1 X_1 + \partial_2 X_2 + \partial_3 X_3 + \ldots + \partial_n X_n + \varphi \quad (5.11)$$

Equation (5.11) is the first stage of the Heckman probit model. Z is the explained variable that is the probability of respondents WTP; X_1,X_2, X_3,... X_n are the explanatory variables, and φ is the residual term.

$$Y = \beta_0 + \beta_1 X_1 + + \beta_2 X_2 + \beta_3 X_3 + \ldots + \beta_n X_n + \delta\lambda + \mu \quad (5.12)$$

Equation (5.12) is the multiple linear regression equation used in the second stage of the Heckman model. Y is the dependent variable which examines the factors affecting the respondents' payment level. The mills' ratio is λ to overcome the sample selection bias (Johnson et al., 2012), β_1, β_2, β_3,...βn and δ are the coefficients to be estimated. X_1, X_2, X_3... X_n are the independent variables, and μ is the residual term. Description and descriptive statistics of the variables used in the model are provided in Table 5.15:

We used Equation (5.12) to estimate the payment level in each zone of the city. The result is provided as:

$$\text{WTP}_{z1} = \sum_{i=1}^{n} \alpha_i Pr_i = 393 \quad (5a)$$

$$\text{WTP}_{Z2} = \sum_{i=1}^{n} \alpha_i Pr_i = 534 \quad (5b)$$

$$\text{WTP}_{Z3} = \sum_{i=1}^{n} \alpha_i Pr_i = 499 \quad (5c)$$

$$\text{WTP}_{Z4} = \sum_{i=1}^{n} \alpha_i Pr_i = 288 \quad (5d)$$

$$\text{WTP}_{\text{All}} = \sum_{i=1}^{n} \alpha_i Pr_i = 376 \quad (5e)$$

The result from (a) to (e) can be inferred that in Zone 2, the willingness to pay is highest with Rs. 534/person per year and least in Zone 4 with Rs. 288/person per year. Zone 1 and Zone 3 have the WTP value of Rs. 393 and Rs. 499/person per year, respectively. This result indicates that the zone with the highest $PM_{2.5}$ level (Table 5.12) and the highest per capita income would be willing to pay the higher amount as compared to other zones. At the aggregate level, the average WTP from the sample survey stands as Rs. 376/person/year.

Heckman's two-step model is applied using Stata 10.1. It should be noted that the probit model in Table 5.10 has 14 explanatory variables (first stage) and 10 explanatory variables[13] are introduced in the second stage (Table 5.11).

Table 5.10 First-stage probit analysis: Factors affecting WTP

Variables	*WTP (Yes = 1; No = 0)*	
	Coefficient	*Z (Std. Error)*
Gender	0.103	0.188
Dage2	0.974[a]	0.247
Dage3	0.786[b]	0.418
Income	0.002[a]	0.001
Dedu2	0.640[a]	0.230
Dedu3	0.419[c]	0.274
Exposure	0.021[a]	0.006
Traffic illness	0.490[a]	0.243
Treatment	0.539[b]	0.229
Awareness	0.502[b]	0.257
WDL	0.032	0.020
Z2	0.358	0.310
Z3	−0.810[a]	0.295
Z4	−1.336[a]	0.281
Constant	0.386	0.471

[a]Significant at 1% level; [b] Significant at 5% level; [c]Significant at 10% level.

Table 5.11 Multiple linear regression analysis: Factors affecting WTP amount

Variables	*WTP amount*	
	Coefficient	*Z (Std. Error)*
Gender	−5.328	39.339
Income	0.006[a]	0.0008
Dedu2	113.604[b]	58.033
Dedu3	163.921[a]	61.764
Traffic illness	144.754[a]	54.770
Awareness	124.405[b]	56.799
WDL	68.310[b]	38.104
Z2	89.591[b]	49.207
Z3	−30.864	56.732
Z4	78.530	61.926
Constant	113.071	89.707
λ	48.167	97.610

Source: Authors' calculation based on a primary survey.
[a]Significant at 1% level; [b]Significant at 5% level; [c]Significant at 10%level

This is because Heckman's model should include at least one variable in the first stage that is different from the variables included in the second stage (Baum, 2006). Based on this principle, the second stage is regressed with statistically significant variables. The value of Wald test is 112.96 and P-valuc is zero, indicating the whole model is effective in explaining the dependent variable.

5.5.5.3 Factors Affecting WTP: Probit Model

The probit model in Table 5.10 explains that the WTP is significantly influenced by income, education level, age, exposure, traffic-related illness, treatment, awareness, and zonal dummy variables. Though the gender variable has a positive sign, it is not statistically significant. Even studies on WTP in relation to air pollution like Alberni et al. (1997) reveal similar results. The age dummy variables, namely, dage2 and dage3, are found to be statistically significant with the positive coefficient sign. This infers those respondents with higher age groups, here who belong to the age group of 26–45 years and 46 years and above are more likely to reveal their willingness to pay for the reduction in traffic-induced air pollution as compared to the base category of respondents who are below the age group of 25 years.

Likewise, the income variable is found to be statistically significant, and the coefficient is positive, which infers those respondents with higher income have stronger WTP for a reduction in traffic-induced air pollution. This is expected theoretically and observed by other studies like Abdullah and Jeanty (2011) and Del Salazan et al. (2015). In a similar manner, the education variables in their dummies viz., dedu2 and dedu3 are positive and statistically significant in explaining the factors affecting the WTP. This indicates that respondents who belong to education category of graduation and above are more likely to pay for the reduction in traffic-induced air pollution as compared to the respondents who belong to education category of less than graduation.[14]

One of the key variables of our study is the traffic exposure variable. This variable is statistically significant at 1 per cent, and its coefficient has a positive sign. The respondents who are exposed to longer duration to the traffic emissions are more likely to provide their WTP for the reduction of the same. Similarly, the traffic-related variables like, the respondents suffering from any traffic-related illness (like cough, asthma, respiratory infections) and respondents who have taken treatment for any such illness, are found statistically significant, and the coefficient is positive. This means respondents who suffer from any such illness and who undergo treatment for the same have a higher probability to reveal their WTP for the reduction of traffic emissions in the city.

The findings from Del Salazon et al. (2015) explained that awareness regarding the implications of air pollution might have a significant impact on the WTP values. A similar result is found in our study. The awareness variable is found statistically significant with a positive coefficient sign. This indicates that respondents who are aware of the traffic-related illness due to traffic emission are more likely to provide their WTP as compared to those who are not aware of the same. Another important variable for the study is the zonal dummies. The coefficients of Zones 3 and 4 are found statistically significant with a negative sign. This infers that the respondents who belong to these zones (3 and 4) are less likely to provide their WTP as compared to respondents who belong to Zone 1. This may be related to comparatively low income level as against respondents of Zone 1.

5.5.5.4 Factors Affecting Payment Levels: Multiple Linear Regression Model

The multiple linear regression model in Table 5.11 indicates that income, education, traffic illness, awareness, and WDL are found statistically significant in relation to the WTP amount. The income variable has a positive coefficient and found statistically significant with WTP amount. This indicates that as income increases, the payment level (WTP amounts) may also increase. In a similar line, education variables have a statistical significance with WTP amounts. The positive sign for these variables (dedu2 and dedu3) indicate that the respondents who belong to higher educational qualification (mainly graduation and post-graduation and above) are more willing to pay a higher amount for the reduction of traffic-induced air pollution, as compared to the respondents with education qualification less than graduation.

Similarly, the respondents who are suffering from any sort of traffic-related illness are willing to pay higher amounts to reduce traffic-induced air pollution. The work-days loss is found statistically significant with a positive sign indicating respondent who faces a high number of days of work loss would like to provide higher amounts of their WTP. The reason may be that respondents with the illness and who lose their work-days may perceive that any reduction in traffic emission may improve their health status and work productivity. On the other hand, respondents who are aware of the traffic-related impacts of the health and environment provide higher amounts of WTP as compared to respondents who are not. The zonal variables are found insignificant in influencing the payment level of WTP.

The inverse mills ratio (λ) is positive and not statistically significant from zero suggesting that there is no sample selection bias in the model. These results are found consistent with the other studies related to air pollution (Alberni et al., 1997; Landefeld & Seskin, 1982; Vlavhokostas et al., 2011).

5.5.6 Estimates of the Economic Cost of Mortality due to Traffic Congestion

Mortality due to traffic-induced air pollution requires careful examination of various factors like population under study, pollutants' impact, nature of the microenvironment (traffic junctions or roadside), age of the population, duration of exposure etc. Even if all these information are available, attaching a monetary value involves methodological complications. The contingent valuation methods are the most popular methods used in the estimation of thc valuc of mortality. It involves estimating mean WTP from the sample for a reduction in traffic-related air pollution and related mortality. The study estimated the economic cost of mortality for traffic-related air pollution based on Equation (5.4).

The annual mean WTP of the study area is estimated as Rs. 376 per person and jointly, the average WTP for the sample would be Rs. 1,60,552. The value represents an aggregation of individual values for a small change in risk of death. The risk of death is estimated as 910 (0.018%). The economic cost of traffic-induced mortality can be estimated as Rs. 14.61 crores for the year 2018–2019. This cost accounts for almost 0.03 per cent of the city's GDP (2018–2019).

One major limitation of the analysis is it cannot combine the cost of mortality and morbidity to derive total health cost. This is due to methodological complications as morbidity costs are derived from the revealed preference method (COI), and mortality costs are derived from stated preference method (CVM).

5.6 Conclusion

A novel effort is made to estimate health and productivity impacts due to traffic congestion. $PM_{2.5}$ being the primary pollutant from vehicular emissions tends to have varying health impacts from headache to major issues like respiratory infections and asthma issues.

Key variables like total exposure and $PM_{2.5}$ are found to have a significant and positive impact on traffic-related illness. A key finding is that the impact of mode of transportation on the health issue. It is found that two-wheeler users are more likely to suffer from the risk of respiratory infection as compared to car users. In the case of mortality, the study estimated that 10$\mu g/m^3$ decrease in $PM_{2.5}$ would reduce the traffic-induced mortality by 0.018 per cent.

Using the Heckman's two-step model, it is found that income, education, and other traffic-related variables are statistically significant in influencing the WTP and payment levels. From the empirical result, we found that respondents who are aware of the issue are more likely to contribute to the reduction of pollution.

With DRF between the traffic pollutants and health impact, the economic cost of morbidity and mortality is estimated. The morbidity impacts are valued using the COI approach. The average annual direct COI is estimated as Rs. 4,944 per person and an annual indirect COI is Rs. 13,104 per person. Using the CVM method, the study estimated the economic cost of mortality due to traffic-induced air pollution as Rs. 14.61 crores for the city. This is almost 0.03 per cent of the city's GDP (2018–2019).

Notes

1 Industries (20 per cent) and domestic activities (8 per cent).
2 Study of distribution and determinants of health-related events (diseases) (WHO).
3 Criteria pollutants are non-toxic air pollutants (CO, NO_2, PM, SO_2, lead, ozone), an excess concentration of these would be hazardous to health.
4 Other pollutants like SO_2 and NO_2 are found within the standards limit in the city and also there is lack strong evidence of their health impact being the independent variable (HEI, 2010).
5 The data are controlled for smoking habits among respondents.
6 Stress is considered as a leading factor of illness and as an illness per se.
7 The values do not add up to 100% due to multiple responses in each group.
8 Travelling for the work-place in the city. Since this variable correlated with age as the respondents are working population, we have not considered the age variable in the model to avoid multicollinearity.
9 YTR_3 is not significant, which can be attributed to closer category.
10 Since the economic estimation of intangible costs is highly subjective, the present study estimated two major costs.
11 These costs do not include any major medical investigation costs.
12 Preventive measures are not added for aggregation.
13 As other variables are not found significant.
14 Further, it is found in the literature that graduates and higher-than graduate commuters tend to travel more than the commuters with less education than graduation.

References

Abdullah, S., & Jeanty, W. P. (2011). Willingness to pay for renewable energy: Evidence from a contingent valuation survey in Kenya. *Renewable and Sustainable Energy Reviews*, *15*(6), 2974–2983.

Adams, H. S., Kenny, L. C., Nieuwenhuijsen, M. J., Colvile, R. N., & Gussman, R. A. (2001). Design and validation of a high flow personal sampler for $PM_{2.5}$. *Journal of Exposure Analysis and Environmental Epidemiology*, *11*(1), 5–11.

Alberni, A., Cropper, M., Tsu-Tan, F., Krupnick, A., Liu, J. T., Shaw, D., & Harrington, W. (1997). Valuing health effects of air pollution in developing countries: The case of Taiwan. *Journal of Environmental Economics and Management*, *34*(2), 107–126.

AQEG (Air Quality Expert Group). (2012). Fine Particulate Matter ($PM_{2.5}$) in the United Kingdom. Prepared for the Department of Environment, Food And Rural Affairs; Scottish Executive; Welsh Government; And Department Of The Environment In The Northern Ireland. London: Defra. www.gov.uk/government/uploads/system/uploads/attachment_data/file/69635/pb13837-aqeg-fine-particle-matter-20121220.pdf

Auto Fuel Policy. (2014). Auto fuel vision and vision 2025. Retrieved June 27, 2019, from http://petroleum.nic.in/sites/default/files/autopol.pdf

Balarajan, R., & McDowall, M. R. (1988). Professional drivers in London: A mortality study. *British Journal of Industrial Medicine*, *45*(7), 483–486.

Balashanmugam, P., Nehrukumar, V., & Balasubranian, G. (2015). Assessment of Semi-urban air pollution and its health impacts due to vehicular traffic emissions in Chdambaram Town, Tamilnadu, India. *International Journal of Scientific Research in Science, Engineering and Technology*, *1*(6), 12–21.

Baum, C. F. (2006). *An introduction to modern econometrics using Stata*. Stata Press.

Chan, C. C., Ozkaynak, H., Spengler, J. D., & Sheldon, L. (1991). Diver exposure to volatile organic compounds, CO, Ozone and NO_2 under different driving conditions. *Environmental Science and Technology*, *25*(5), 964–972.

COMEAP (Committee on the Medical Effects of Air Pollutants). (2009). Long term exposure to air pollution: Effect on mortality. A report by COMEAP. Health Protection Agency. Retrieved August 22, 2019, from www.comeap.org.uk/images/storeis/documents/reports/mortality%20report$202009.pdf

COMEAP (Committee on the Medical Effects of Air Pollutants). (2011). The mortality effects of long-term exposure to particulate air pollution in the United Kingdom. A report by COMEAP. Health Protection Agency. Retrieved August 28, 2019, from www.hpa.org.uk/webc/hpawebfiel/hpaweb_c/1317137012567

CPCB (Central Pollution Control Board). (2011). Air quality monitoring, emissioninventory and source apportionment study for Indian cities. www.indiaenvironmentportal.org.in

Cropper, M. L., Simon, N. B., Alberini, A., Arora, S., & Sharma, P. K. (1997). The health benefits of air pollution control in Delhi. *American Journal of Agricultural Economics*, *79*(5), 1625–1629.

Cropper, M. L., & Freeman, A. M. (1991). Environmental health effects. In J. B. Braden & C. Kolstad (Eds.), *Measuring the demand for environmental quality*. Elsevier Science Publishers.

Del Salazan, S., Gonzάlez-Gómez, F., & Guardiola, F. (2015). Willingness to pay toimprove urban water supply: The case of Sucre, Bolivia. *Water Policy*, *17*(1), 112–125.

Health Effect Institute (HEI). (2010). Traffic-related air pollution: A critical review of the literature on emission, exposure and health effects. HEI Special Report 17. Health Effect Institute.

Dewaram, W., Spengler, J. D., & Schwartz, J. (1997). Valuing environmental cost in India: The economy wide impact of environmental degradation. *Environmental Research*, *59*, 362–373.

Health Effect Institute (HEI). (2019). State of global air 2019: A special report on global exposure to air pollution and its disease burden. HEI.

Jerrett, M., Brunett, R. T., Ma, R., Pope III, C. A., Krewski, D., Newbold, K. B., Thurston, G., Shi, Y., Finkelstein, N., Calle, E. E., & Thun, M. J. (2005). Spatial analysis of air pollution and mortality in Los Angeles. *Epidemiology*, *16*, 727–736.

Johnson, B. K., Whitehead, J. C., Mason, D. S., & Walker, G. J. (2012). Willingess to pay for downtown public goods generated by large, sportes-anchored development projects: The CVM approach. *City, Culture and Society*, *3*, 201–208.

Kaur, S., et al. (2005). Personal exposure of street canyon intersection users to $PM_{2.5}$, ultrafine particle counts and carbon monoxide in Central London, UK. *Atmospheric Environment*, *39*, 3629–3641.

Kong, F., Xiong, K., & Zhang, N. (2014). Determinants of Farmers' willingness to pay and its level for ecological compensation of Poyang Lake Wetland, China: A household-level survey. *Sustainability*, *6*, 6714–6728. https://doi.org/10.3390/su6106714

Landefeld, S. J., & Seskin, P. E. (1982). The economic value of life: Linking theory to practice. *American Journal of Public Health*, *72*(6), 555–565.

Lave, L. B., & Seskin, E. P. (1970). Air pollution and human health. *Science*, *169*, 723–733.

Lave, L. B., & Seskin, E. P. (1973). An analysis of the association between U.S. Mortality and air pollution. *Journal of American Statistical Association*, *68*, 284–290.

McCubbin, R. D., & Delucci, M. A. (1999). The health cost of motor vehicle related air pollution. *Journal of Transport Economics and Policy*, *33*(3), 253–286.

OECD (Organization for Economic Co-Operation and Development). (2014). The cost of air pollution: Health impacts of road transport. OECD Publishing. http://doi.org/10.1787/9789264210448-en

NHSRC (National Health System Resource Centre). (2018). Vital statistics of Karnataka based on the civil registration system 2016–17. http://nhsrcindia.org/

Parikh, J. K. (2004). *Valuing the health impacts of air pollution: Environmental economics in practice: Case studies from India* (pp. 240–267). Oxford University Press.

Pervin, T., Gerdtham, G., & Lyttkens, C. H. (2008). Societal cost of air pollution-related health hazards: A review of methods and results. *Cost Effectiveness and Resource Allocation*, *6*(19). www.Resoure-Allocation.Com/Content/6/1/19

Schwartz, J., & Zeger, S. (1990). Passive smoking, air pollution and acute respiratory symptoms in a diary study of student nurses. *American Review of Respiratory Disease*, *141*(1), 62–67.

Schwartz, J., et al. (2002). The concentration-response relation between PM2.5 and daily death. *Environmental Health Perspectives*, *110*(10), 1025–1029.

Small, K. (1977). Air pollution cost of transport modes. *Journal of Transport Economics and Policy*, *11*(2), 109–132.

Stern, F. B., Halperin, W. E., Hornung, R. W., Ringenburg, V. L., & Mccammon, C. S. (1988). Heart disease mortality among bridge and tunnel officers exposure to carbon monoxide. *American Journal of Epidemiology*, *128*(6), 1276–1288.

Vlachokostas, C., Achillas, C., Slini, T., Moussiopoulous, N., Banias, G., & Dimitrakis, R. (2011). Willingness to pay for reducing the risk of premature mortality attributed to air pollution: A contingent valuation study for Greece. *Atmospheric Pollution Research*, *2*(3), 275–282.

The Energy and Resource Institute (TERI). (2015). Air pollution and health. Discussion Paper by the Energy and Resource Institute: New Delhi. TERI.

WHO (World Health Organization). (2005). *Health effects of transport-related air pollution* (Michal Krzyanowski, Birgir Kuna-Dibbert & Jurgen Schneider, Eds.). WHO Regional Office for Europe.

WHO (World Health Organization). (2013). Review of evidence on health aspects of air pollution: REVIHAAP project. Technical report. WHO Regional office for Europe. www.euro.who.int/__data/assets/pdf_file/0004/193108/REVIHAAP-Final-technical-report-final-version.pdf

WHO Regional Office for Europe, OECD. (2015). Economic cost of health impact of air pollution in Europe: Clean air, health and wealth. WHO Regional Office for Europe.

World Bank. (1997). Valuating the economic impacts of urban environmental problems: Asian Cities. Shin, et al. Working Paper Series 13. Urban Management and poverty reduction.

Chapter 6

Economic Instruments for Traffic Management

6.1 Introduction

The main purpose of economic valuation of externality is to reveal its true costs on society. This directs the policymakers to frame measures, which would internalize these externalities (Mourato, 1998). Earlier chapters have revealed such costs due to traffic congestion externalities in the form of direct and indirect economic costs. As arriving at the true societal costs of congestion has been a challenging task, the same holds true even in the case of framing optimal policy strategies to internalize its externalities. An optimal congestion mitigating strategy is expected to internalize two distinct types of externalities, namely, intra and inter-sectoral. One is with respect to the open-access property of the road-use (intra-sectoral) and other is in relation to environmental pollution (inter-sectoral). The conundrum of policy implementation arises due to the interplay of both the externalities simultaneously. The choice of instrument is expected to bring a behavioural change which results in decongesting the city and betterment of environmental condition together.

In a country like India, internalizing the impact of externalities becomes furthermore challenging for the policymakers. This is mainly due to the interaction of certain strong confounding factors like inadequate infrastructure investments coupled with increasing purchasing behaviour (of automobile) and lack of systematized governance.

Apart from this, developing countries usually follow the solutions applied in developed world. But such ready-made solutions do not yield desired result. For instance, a popular policy strategy advocated by developed countries is to implement the Congestion Pricing system. But this measure has many debates and is also backed up by political and public antagonism. Further, experiences around the world have proved that there is no single direct solution to internalize the externalities of traffic congestion as the problem itself has many complex dimensions. Hence, it requires a cautious examination of various policies which could suit the needs of the area under study.

DOI: 10.4324/9781032662299-6

In this background, we examine the effectiveness of various policy instruments in internalizing the traffic congestion externalities. Both international and national level best practices will be reviewed. Based on our field survey, we also derived the public perceptions on these policies.

6.2 Instruments to Internalize the Traffic Congestion Externalities

The policy measures to address traffic congestion can be broadly classified into common-and-control measures and economic incentives. The former tries to specify the mandatory actions such as placing limits on activities, whereas the latter persuades the behaviour indirectly by altering the incentive structure in the market (Gomez, 1998). As the traffic congestion externalities pose a complex challenge due to the interplay of the externalities, the policy instruments to internalize these externalities need to be chosen carefully. Such an act requires proper analysis of the instruments suitable for the problem under study.

6.2.1 *Command and Control Measures (CAC)*

Command and control regime involves predominant and traditional forms of regulations. The basic idea of these regulations is to make the society to fall into the prescribed norms. The policy presupposes strict and consistent measures that are feasible, acceptable, and enforceable (Nijkamp & Shefer, 1998). Command and control regulations may take various forms like specific fines, penalties, emission control equipment requirement, emission limit, etc.

The major advantage of CAC measures lies in its flexibility in regulating any complex issue and more certainty in policy outcome. The regulatory measures of CAC became quite popular due to the simplified monitoring of compliance.

Although CAC measures bear certain advantages, there are some drawbacks. For example, CAC measures do not satisfy the equi-marginal principle. It is quite not possible for CAC instruments to ensure that the marginal costs of pollution control are equalized among different polluters who are contributing to the same level of pollution (Kolstad, 2000). Further, CAC measures provide weak incentives for innovation (Jaffe & Stavins, 1995). The major difference between CAC measures and economic incentives are (a) there is a restricted choice for the polluter to achieve the set target by the regulator and (b) a lack of mechanisms for equalizing marginal control costs among several different polluters (Kolstad, 2000).

6.2.2 *Economic Instruments (EI): Taxonomy*

Economic instruments (EI) aim to bridge the gap between the private and social cost by internalizing all the external costs (Panayotou, 1994). They are ideally suited when the objective of the policy is to reconcile the environmental concerns with development needs and integrate the environmental and economic policies. The main virtues of the instruments are related to their efficiency or cost-minimization objective, flexibility in accommodating heterogeneity, adjustability to changing circumstance, and market correction quality (Panayotou, 1994). If designed and implemented properly, economic instruments have the power to harness the forces of market and self-interest and turn them into powerful allies to foster economic development with environmental protection.

The economic instruments have become popular as measures of sustainable transportation policy (Nijkamp & Shefer, 1998). The idea behind these instruments lies in the credence that the market offers the best available democratic possibilities for alleviating negative externalities by having the users to pay for the damage caused (Gomez-Ibanez & Small, 1994). Economic instruments rely on incentive mechanism than regulations. They provide rewards for individuals to do what is perceived to be in the public interest (Kolstad, 2000). These instruments rely on the market forces to derive prices for the externalities.

Economic instruments to internalize the externalities of traffic congestion can be broadly classified into four measures (refer to Figure 6.1) namely, property rights, market creations, charges, and financial instruments.

a) **Property Rights:** A well-defined, secure, and transferable property rights are observed to ensure proper use of resources or emergence of the market (price). The application of this instrument to traffic congestion externalities takes a different form. Attenuation of property rights through regulation of use are often used to internalize externalities. This can be found as use rights in the form of 'driving license'. Though the acquisition of driving license ensures the eligibility of the user to drive the vehicle, the authority can use the same to restrict the vehicle-use when needed. Restriction on the number of licenses to be issued in a year is a popular method of restricting vehicle users in the country (Button & Verhoef, 1998).

Property Rights	**Market Creation**	**Charge System**	**Financial Instruments**
• Licensing	• Permits	• Pollution Charges/Tax • User Charges/Road Tolls • Betterment Charges	• Subsidies • Soft Loans • Relocation Incentives

Figure 6.1 Economic Instruments to Internalize the Externalities of Traffic Congestion.

Source: Modified from Panayotou (1994).

As many pointed out, property rights are limited in their use with respect to the resources which are mobile. Further, issuing the rights/license involves political contentions through rent-seeking and corruptions. Another major limitation of use rights is on its distributional impacts. Often it may deprive the poor to access the resource unless they are the recipients of property rights. However, the major advantage of the use rights is low transaction costs and easy implementation. Unlike taxes and charges, use rights adjust automatically to changing circumstances.

b) **Market Creation: Permits:** As seen, the use rights or license do not achieve the desired result. They are more effective in internalizing the on-site environmental cost rather than the dynamic external costs. One solution which the State can consider is defining the desired level of environmental quality and creating a market for it (Panayotou, 1994). Creating market can assign the right to use the environment up to a prescribed level through pricing, and these rights can be traded. They are called permits.

A popular form of permit is tradeable emission permits. When these permits are applied to traffic congestion externalities, it can take two different forms aiming at two different externalities of traffic congestion. As observed, traffic congestion is a common phenomenon during peak-hour; permits can take the form of tradeable travel permits during these hours. These permits are issued to private transport users entering the CBD of the city to increase their travel cost. This ensures restricted travel during the peak hour, which reduces congestion by encouraging public transport in the area.

Another form is to set the total supply of permits to achieve a specified target for ambient air quality and congestion reduction. These permits may be sold or distributed through grandfathering. Everyone has a permit to use the car, for instance, three days a week only. When someone wants to use the car for more days, or when he wants to buy a new car, he has to obtain a permit from someone else. The permits can be purchased and sold, leased, rented, or lent. In this way, the total amount of cars used is limited both in the present and the future, as the number of permits is fixed. This system will require a judicious choice of the magnitude of fines and a reasonable probability of being caught should be enough to encourage substantial compliance (Nijakamp & Shefer, 1998). This necessitates a fair amount of administration of all transactions. The danger of this system is the transaction does not take place because of insurmountable transaction costs. The grandfathering of existing vehicles avoids serious political resistance to this mechanism.

c) **Charge System:** Charges are defined as payments for the use of resources or services which are akin to prices of market goods. These charges, sometimes take the form of taxes when applied to environmental resources. For traffic congestion, Pigouvian tax can be defined as a charge imposed on the commuter to the amount of the marginal social cost of his travel activity. In the transport economics literature, this measure is adopted in different names, viz., congestion pricing, road pricing, congestion tax, congestion toll, cordon pricing, etc. Theoretically, this policy-strategy is preferable in a market system where there is good knowledge of commuter behaviour, but its implementation encounters great difficulties, especially in developing countries.

Another form of charge relevant to traffic congestion is user charge, known as road tolls. Generally, road tolls are used to raise the States' revenue. But in many countries, these charges are also used to reduce the congestion of the area. Area licensing system adopted in Singapore can be a good example of this. In this system, entry to the city centre or area is through the paid entry. This measure is expected to decrease the private vehicle ply in the busy areas of the city.

d) **Financial Instruments:** The financial instruments like subsidies, soft loans, and relocation incentives are considered as a second-best policy solution (First-best policy is Road Pricing). In these measures, the users are expected to receive incentives to internalize the externalities.

In case of traffic congestion externalities, it can be understood as the measures to encourage clean-fuel vehicles or incentives to decongest the area in the form of relocation incentives. Including the developing country like India, many countries around the world are promoting the use of clean-fuel vehicles which reduces the pollution, by providing purchase subsidies and soft loans (TERI, 2010; World Bank, 2018). Subsidies are also used to promote public transport system by reducing the travel fares in many countries. In the case of a few Indian cities (like Delhi), major industries or companies are asked to relocate their units to less congested areas so that the city's congestion could be relieved (IIHS, 2015).

6.3 Effectiveness of CAC and Economic Instruments: Global Evidence

There are several CAC and Economic instruments used to regulate urban traffic congestion. The evidence provided here is not exhaustive but provide some guidelines on the implementations of such instruments. Further, a detailed description of each type of instruments is difficult to examine due to the diversity of the objectives aimed by them. For example, subsidizing public transport may seem like a measure to reduce congestion but may also aim to address the affordability issue of low-income class mobility. Hence in this section, a brief outline of the policy measures adopted in different countries and India, in particular, are provided.

6.3.1 Command and Control Policies in Practice

A range of command-and-control instruments are used to curtail the road congestion around the world. This section discusses certain popular evidence.

Car Bans: One of the most popular command and control policy is banning cars from entering certain areas of the city. The most popular form of this measure involves prohibiting the number of vehicles to urban centres using a permit system, which is found in many places like Milan, cities of Australia. A similar impact is also found in case of restricting vehicle entry through number plates (odd/even policy) in Athens and Lagossince 1982. An important side of this policy is the restriction of car ownership. Bermuda (Button & Verhoef, 1998) imposed limits on household to own one car. In Japan, a car license can be obtained, only if there is off-street parking (implemented in Tokyo). In Mexico City, a novel strategy of 'no-driving day' policy was introduced in 1989. The program mandated not to drive in the city for one day during the week (except weekends) and during weekends. The program also used odd–even license plate numbers. This removed 20 per cent of the vehicles from streets in the first month, which improved the air quality (Timilsina & Dulal, 2009). In cities of Switzerland, mainly in Bern and Zurich commuters resorted to use public transport due to restrictive measures on private vehicles (Timilsina & Dulal, 2009).

These measures have faced many issues and failed to contain the growth of traffic congestion in their respective cities. For example, in Athens, the implementation of the odd–even policy has resulted in a high degree of manipulation of car-number plates by scarping and fitting it to vehicles to use the vehicles all over the week (Matsoukis, 1985). In Mexico case, the no-driving day policy did not last long due to the inability of public transport to accommodate the increased travel demand. Further, odd–even policy in Greece (Athens) increased the purchase of second-hand vehicles which increased air pollution (ECMT, 1999). Fraudulent applications for licenses and use of false number plates were common in Lagos (Button & Verhoef, 1998). Even in Tokyo, parking restriction has led to a distortion in house prices which led to undesirable response to residential architecture.

Traffic Management: Physical management of traffic through various measures like traffic lights, one-way streets are traditional methods to ease congestion. Many European cities have traffic cell system, mazes (one-way streets, local closure) or traffic calming zones (speed humps, narrow roads) which are intended to increase the time cost of trip-making of individuals. A study by OECD (1989) reported that in Gothenburg, these measures have diverted the travel from private to public transport (metro trains). In the case of developing countries, such measures may seem costly and often becomes inflexible to operate. Another side of this measure involves a requirement of an effective enforcement mechanism. It is estimated that in London, of 150, 000 parking offences, almost 49,000 go undetected, and many who are caught may not pay the imposed fees (Joseph, 1991).

Land-use Planning: Land-use planning has been a major element in the urban transport policy. The nature and magnitude of travel largely depend on urban land-use planning. Since transport demand is a derived demand, it is possible to influence the travel pattern by re-locating the spatial patterns. This involves the physical concentration of the economic activities and residential setups around which the transport networks would be built. A popular report by the UK Ministry of Transport (1963) called Buchanan Report has recommended for designing the land-use to minimize the private travel. Basing this report, a Dutch strategy has been evolved by locating new commercial development around the major public transport interchanges (Button & Verhoef, 1998). East Germany, on the other hand, being confronted with transport constraints, framed its industrial policy which proposed geographically concentrated industries for its areas which acted as a congestion-calming strategy (Button & Verhoef, 1998). In recent years, land-use planning has evolved as a smart-growth development strategy for transport mobility plans. This involves increasing the density of economic activities which reduces driving, more connected road networks, space-efficient modes, and so on (Litman, 2016).

Land-use planning is rather a long-term strategy to reduce congestion. There are evidence which shows that pedestrianization and car bans produce some beneficial effects in central urban areas. But such measures may also lead to additional traffic in the surrounding areas. Bypass or circular road construction may seem a key component of land-use/transportation planning, which may avoid traffic to the core area. Still, it cannot be considered as a universal solution to traffic congestion. This is seen in London where construction of M25 motorway around the city has attracted considerable and unexpected local traffic. In the case of developing country cities, due to the unplanned nature of the city's growth poses a serious constraint to develop a systematized land-use planning as a congestion-calming strategy.

Parking Charges: Parking charges is intended to reduce the traffic mobility. Caution to be taken before implementing these charges are it has spatial distribution implications by shifting the traffic to less congested streets. It is advocated that zone parking charge area may look feasible, but it may induce fringe parking effects (Gillen, 1977).

Practiced for many years in most cities of developed countries, parking charges are implemented to reduce car use in the central business districts. In the USA, it is estimated that 90 per cent of commuters park their cars free of cost at their workplace (Willson & Shoup, 1990) and 60 per cent of parking is on the off-street facility in UK cities mainly Bristol, Oxford, and Cambridge (Button & Verhoef, 1998). This makes the implementation of parking fee quite difficult. To counter this, in New Zealand, as an anti-congestion measure, the Commission on Environment has implemented terminal fees which make employees pay a tax on free parking provided by the employers (Button & Verhoef, 1998).

It is observed from the cases of Italy and the Netherlands (Ponti & Vittadini, 1990; Vleuget et al., 1990 cited in Button & Verhoef, 1998) that the impact of parking charges in reducing congestion is a variable one in terms of their efficiency. There is a little evidence of public acceptance of high parking fees, and they tend to evade except in the face of heavy enforcement and ipso facto, transaction cost (Button & Verhoef, 1998). This was experienced in London where despite of parking policies, due to the tightening of policing of traffic regulation has reduced the congestion on designated traffic corridors (Button & Verhoef, 1998). The major contention of such policing is it involves huge costs and might favour administration pretence.

6.3.2 Economic Instruments in Practice

As against the CAC measures, economic instruments provide a kind of incentives to persuade the road users to reduce the traffic congestion externalities. Some of the major instruments are discussed in this section.

Vehicle Taxation: In some countries, fixed charges like vehicle tax have been implemented as their congestion reduction policy. Hong Kong, for example, has trebled annual car tax in 1982 and doubled its purchase tax. This has reduced their car ownership by 20 per cent in the following years (Button & Verhoef, 1998). In Singapore, taxes in the form of registration fees and annual license fees are made to amount up to two-third of the purchase price of a car. The aim was to reduce the car ownership growth.

Another innovative form of this measure was introduced in Singapore in the form of differential licenses. The mechanism has allowed the use of a car during low congestion periods. For example, if a new car is to be used at weekends when the congestion is less, then there is preferential treatment in the form of lower fees. The impact of such a measure is ambiguous due to traceability problems.

Fuel Taxation: Increasing fuel taxes is advocated as a measure to control congestion even by those who keep road pricing as a superior policy instrument (Mohring, 1989). Often many countries, including Singapore, use it as a congestion reduction policy. In the case of developing countries like India, such an increase in fuel tax may have other repercussion effects, which may lead to distribution impacts.

Improvement and Subsidies to Public Transport: Subsidizing public transport aims to attract road users away from their vehicles. It is widely used in European countries. For instance, in the Netherlands, more than 65 per cent of the public transport cost has been subsidized. The main caution to be taken in such measure is to manage the subsidy flow more efficiently and for specific objective for which it is aimed for (Button & Costa, 1997). In the light of subsidizing the public transport, investment, and subsidization of another congestion-reducing form of transport: light rapid transit system gained popularity in recent years (Litman, 2016). These are long-term approaches which often hoped to reduce congestion.

Research studies indicated that public transit improvement would reduce private vehicle trips. Ewing et al. (2014) investigated the impact of a light-rail system (LRT) in Salt Lake City, which began operating in 2001 and expanded over the following decade. The study estimated that the LRT line reduced daily vehicle traffic on the study corridor about 50 per cent (from 44,000 to 22,300 trips). Bhattacharjee and Goetz (2012) found that Denver traffic volumes grew 31 per cent in vehicle metre travelled (VMT) inside the light-rail corridor, but increased VMT outside the corridor by 41 per cent between 1992 and 2008. Similarly, Jeihani et al. (2013) while evaluating the impact of transit-oriented development (TOD) in Washington D.C. and Baltimore metropolitan region found that regional traffic reduced by 1.2 per cent and 2.8 per cent due to TOD. Residents relied more on public transport and walking, which led to a 20 per cent reduction in the annual miles undertaken as compared to other regions.

A mere subsidy to enhance the public transport and expecting the modal shift may not be an economically viable strategy. An optimal traffic management policy should include co-existence of both road pricing and subsidized public transport network (Litman, 2016). Sherman in 1972 itself argued that mere transit subsidy acts as a partial solution to congestion in the absence of road pricing.

Road Pricing: This is held to be the 'First-best policy' solution to calm the traffic congestion. This policy aims at altering the travel behaviour by charging a fee where there is insufficient road capacity to accommodate the travel demand (Small & Gomez-Ibañez, 1998).

Road pricing has taken different forms over the years, viz., area licensing, toll roads, parking taxes etc. In some countries, interest in road pricing has been stimulated by the desire to find new revenue sources for transportation investment and simultaneous failure of alternative policies (Gomez-Ibañez & Small, 1998). Some practical experiences of forms of road pricing are:

a. Singapore's Area Licensing scheme in 1998.
b. Hong Kong's Electronic Road Pricing (ERP) in 1983–1985.
c. Cambridge's Congestion Charging: Metering and Cordon Charges in 1990.
d. Urban Toll Rings in Norway in 1996–1997.
e. Stockholm's Road Pricing in 1991.
f. Road Pricing in the Netherlands in 1980s.
g. London's Congestion Charging in 1970s.

Though experiences around the world shows that it can be an optimal strategy, some cities have faced certain issues with the scheme. For instance, São Paulo city council of Brazil approved for congestion pricing based on the license plate. The public opposed the scheme and opined that metro extension would be a better measure to reduce traffic congestion than pricing. In Edinburgh, due to public opposition, the pricing was rejected in 2002. In 2007, New York City denied the imposition of pricing in Manhattan.

6.3.3 Road Pricing as a Sub-Optimal Strategy

Many economists argued for Pigou's (1920) idea of road pricing to attain an optimal traffic condition in cities. But this may not be the case for every city. Pricing involves high transaction costs, which makes it sub-optimal and often leads to distributional consequences in terms of welfare criteria, making it socially unacceptable. The scope of the present study is not to delve into the theoretical complexities of road pricing, but at the outset, to point at certain caveats of its practical application in developing countries.

Under road pricing the price levied implicitly assumes that full marginal cost pricing is covered. But the calculation of such pricing is complicated due to complexities and heterogeneity of traffic flows. Further, implementation of road pricing requires extensive knowledge about the congestion level in all parts of the transportation network simultaneously, and prediction on travel behaviour (Baxbaum, 2009). It is identified by Vickrey (1969) that, the decision to travel is made at the beginning of a trip, but the impact of travel (congestion) is felt during the route taken and persist even after the trip ends (health impacts). This actually complicates the impact assessment.

Further, the road pricing neglects transaction costs involved in implementing and enforcing the measure. Though the road pricing implemented for the first time in Singapore (Area licensing system) and Norwegian cities (cordon pricing) have found it is relatively cheaper to implement, but they lack spatial and temporal sensitivity (Button & Verhoef, 1998). Technological advancement in recent years in the form of 'smart cards' or 'license cards' as a means of automatic payment called electronic road pricing, have reduced these transaction costs. But there always exists a threat to personal privacy. Even in the implementation of e-pricing, a high amount of transaction costs is involved in the maintenance of centralized data collection and state-of-the-art technological updates in the entire complex transport networks.

Further, the nature and severity of the problem of traffic congestion are more complex now than during the time of Pigou (Arnott et al., 1990). Major complication faced in the implementation of road pricing is that unless the entire network is priced, motorists often shift their travel to un-priced route, making the congestion to spread to the entire network, thus reducing overall welfare. At another level, there might be political concerns and public unattractiveness.

6.3.4 Road Pricing and Equity Impacts

The early studies on traffic congestion have paid little attention to its equity impacts on different classes of the road users. The major complication of road pricing is the creation of many direct losers (Thomson, 1998). Most road users may get worse-off as the price paid is more than the value of their congestion savings (otherwise there would be no traffic reduction).

Devised for better management of scarce road use, the pricing would favour those groups of road users who place high value for the time savings (Arnott et al., 1994). Mainly there are three distributional impacts of road pricing: one is quite straight forward, those who value the time savings highly, will either benefit more than what they pay or will feel that they are receiving too little for their money (Thomson, 1998). Secondly, if there is an alternative road (without pricing/toll), the traffic-flow will divert to such road, further aggravating the congestion elsewhere in the network. Lastly, those who are not vehicle owners at present, desire to do so in future, on whom the pricing will place a high shadow price for not allowing them to realize their objective (Button & Verhoef, 1998). Since road pricing does not distinguish the users based on their income status, it would generally lead to welfare loss of those who could not afford the road.

Another argument highlighted by the Public Choice School of economic thought is on the revenue collection. Potentially, any charging system can be treated as a pure sumptuary tax by the public. There may also be concern about the ways in which the revenues from pricing might be spent. It is advocated that the revenue from the road pricing should be used to compensate the losers, but in practice, this is most unlikely to happen (Thomson, 1998). Although road pricing can produce an economically efficient solution to road congestion, travellers may find it as a burden if the revenues are not used to increase mobility (Buxbaum, 2009).

When congestion pricing was developed as the first-best solution it is based on the assumption that the optimal price of road space is equal to the marginal cost price (Arnott et al., 1994). But in the real world, the actual implementation of road pricing is regarded as a second-best solution or proxy mechanism. A true social cost pricing is only theoretical and eluded of real-world implementation.

Parking Incentives: California experimented with a cash-out policy for employees of some MNCs. The strategy aims at providing cash equivalent of parking expenses to the employees who do not use the office parking (Kockelman, 2004). This measure reduced the drive-alone cars in the city drastically. Such measures require an effective travel demand management mechanism.

Replacement to Travel: As travel is considered to have a derived demand, advocates of the modern world suggest adopting alternative ways instead of commuting. Particularly in the light of advancement of telecommunication, a replacement of personal trip-making is found attractive. For example, videoconferencing, work-from-home, teleshopping, telecommuting, etc.

6.4 Internalization of Externalities of Traffic Congestion: Indian Experiences

Like most of the countries, India too followed the traditional approach of handling traffic-flow on the road space. Road expansion as a measure to ease mobility has been in practice and viewed as an optimal strategy. Certain policy measures taken to decongest the cities (apart from investment in public transport) are found in certain metropolitan cities like Delhi, Mumbai, and Bengaluru. In this section, the study attempted to provide evidence of decongestion strategies and pollution reduction measures adopted by the cities of India. Further, there is a thin line of difference between the decongestion policies and pollution reduction measures due to overlapping impacts. For instance, car bans in the city centre not only reduce congestion but also improves air quality. Hence, this section does not make such classification but provides the strategies adopted by the Indian cities. As road transport falls under the State subject, various cities have adopted different types of strategies suitable for their area.

Awarded as one of the most polluted cities in the country, Delhi has taken various initiatives. In 1990, Delhi government and Central Petroleum Ministry mandated the installation of catalytic converters (CC) in automobiles. In 1995, Delhi government introduced a subsidy for the installation of CC in all two and three-wheelers. In 1998, the ministry announced the extension of this to all cities. A study examined the level of air quality after the installation of CC in Delhi by taking five-year data after the policy and found that there is a significant decline in PM and SO_2 by 19 per cent and 69 per cent, respectively (Greenstone et al., 2017).

To decongest the city, Delhi experimented the policy called 'Odd–even' to restrict the private car drivers entering the central zone during peak hours in 2015. The policy did not receive public acceptance, and hence the transport department reverted the policy. In the meantime, the city has invested in building metro lines for the city.

In the case of the study area, Bengaluru, a popular decongesting policy followed is to build more road capacities. Due to the ever-expanding nature of the city, many flyovers, expansion of the existing roads and corridors were undertaken. The city also invested in the construction of Metro line in 2004 itself with an initial estimated project cost of around Rs. 26405.14 crores. The first phase was completed in 2010, and the second phase in 2016, both the phases are catering to the needs of the city's mobility partially. Due to the high operational cost involved, the ticket fares are comparatively high in metro trains, which made it unattractive. Further, to promote public transportation, the city also announced the implementation of sub-urban trains, but the project is still under implementation process.

As a pilot study, an incentive mechanism is initiated for Infosys employees in Bengaluru to travel in uncongested time. The study found a significant improvement in employee's productivity and on-time arrivals due to the incentive. Even the occupancy in company buses also improved (Merugu et al., 2019). Such incentives can be adopted by the large companies for their employees.

One of the most debated policies of Government of India is Smart city Mission launched in 2015. The key strategy of this mission is to develop cities with sustainable mobility. This mainly achieved by developing environmentally friendly, compact cities with more insistence on non-motorized transport. Bengaluru city has got the recognition into the smart city status, but the measures towards decongesting the city are yet to get a proper framework.

The role of city traffic police department in managing the traffic has been very crucial. The department identified 15 junctions in the city as 'zero-tolerance junctions' which are high traffic density junctions. These junctions are under strict surveillance. Implementing one-ways and parking restriction in the city centre are the popular measures in the city. To improve compliance, the city's traffic department introduced a mobile app called 'Publiceye' in 2015, which enabled public participation in identifying the traffic violation. With this, the police department received more than one lakh violations (as on Dec. 2019) as observed by the public and the department also taken necessary action against the violators.

As a pilot effort, the city implemented 'dedicated bus lane' in outer ring road in 2019 and seen the performance of the traffic. It is observed that the speed of buses in the pilot period increased to 18–20 kms from 10 kms. But, this effort faced certain on-road issues with respect to handling the traffic flow with the lane (as the city lacks proper land-use planning).

6.4.1 Measures to Reduce Vehicular pollution

There is good number of laws pertaining to controlling the vehicular pollution than the vehicular ownership in India. This section provides a glimpse of the existing laws on pollution control mechanisms in India.

a. **Air Act:** Section 20 of the act specifies some standards for the emissions from automobiles to be laid down by State Board. Under clause (g) of sub-section (1) of Section 17, the State Government shall, in consultation with State Board, give instructions to the concerned authority in charge of registration of motor vehicles under Motor Vehicle Act, 1988 regarding the standard to be set.
b. **Motor Vehicle Act, 1988:** The amendment to the Act in 1994 encouraged the usage of CNG as fuel and as an incentive permit to encourage clean vehicles. The amendment in the year 2000 authorized the use of LPG as an automotive fuel.

6.4.2 *Role of Judiciary on Vehicular Air Pollution*

The Supreme Court has given the Right to Live in a healthy environment as a fundamental right under Article 21 of the Constitution of India. The first case which addressed the vehicular pollution in the court of law was Murali Purushothaman vs. Union of India[1] where the petitioner brought out the consequences of air pollution by automobile and urged the court to standardize the statutory measures to reduce the pollutants from vehicles (Shekhar, 2015). The court directed the State Government to take appropriate measures to implement Rule 115 and Rule 116 of Motor Vehicles Rules and to expedite the process of installation of necessary equipment for monitory air quality. Various orders passed by the Supreme Court so far can be summed up as:

- Use and sale of leaded petrol are banned.
- Phase-wise removal of old commercial and transport vehicles were ordered.
- Ban on use of two-stroke oil.
- Two-stroke engines were provided with pre-mix petrol.
- Two independent fuel testing laboratories are to be established.
- Euro I norm for non-commercial vehicles was made mandatory and subsequently Euro II by 2000. Proposal to implement Euro V.
- Expansion of CNG outlets.
- Augmenting public transport system.
- Phasing out of commercial/transport vehicles older than 15 years.
- Replacement of all pre-1990 auto and taxi with clean fuels.
- Conversion of entire bus-fleet (public and private) to use CNG in Delhi.
- In 2015, the Hon'ble court mandated the implementation of Environmental Compensation Charge for Commercial vehicles entering the Delhi city. In the same year, the court banned the registration of new diesel cars (larger than 2000cc) till March 2016.
- In 2016, the Delhi government restricted the entry of trucks during peak hour and allowed entry between 9 PM–11 PM.

Emission Norms in India: The first effective norm came into existence in 1989. This got replaced soon with new sets of rules in 1991 for petrol and diesel emissions in 1992. Most vehicle manufacturers had to incorporate technology upgradation such as catalytic converter to reduce exhaust emission. This necessitated the use of lead-free and low sulphur fuels (Shekhar, 2015). From the year 2000, the country adopted the EU standard, Euro I and II norms. In 2003, the Auto Fuel Policy was introduced to harmonize the vehicle regulations in the country and adoption of Europe standard for tighter fuel quality and emission standard.

6.5 Public Perception of the Probable Policies to Internalize the Externalities

As a part of the primary survey, the study elicited the causes and probable policy options for reducing traffic congestion as perceived by the commuters of the city. This would give an idea about the policy strategies to be adopted by the policymakers in decongesting and improving the air quality in the city.

Among the respondents, majority of them (36%) reported that the main cause of traffic congestion in the city is too many private vehicles on the road, and mainly the single-occupant private vehicles. Even slow-moving vehicles like trucks are allowed during the peak-hour on the city's major roads which are causing traffic gridlocks. Figure 6.2 provides the details on the causes of traffic congestion in the city as reported by the respondents.

The primary survey elicited the probable measures to decongest the city. The respondents provided their opinion on the various measures, which included imposing congestion pricing to the expansion of road capacity. It is interesting to know that commuters in the city are aware that certain policies like expansion of road capacity and odd-even policies do not decongests the city. Instead, the majority of the respondents preferred improving the public transport infrastructure and also restricting the single-occupant vehicles on the busy roads of the city as viable strategies. The respondents are also keen on reducing ticket fare of public transport (both bus and metro). To examine

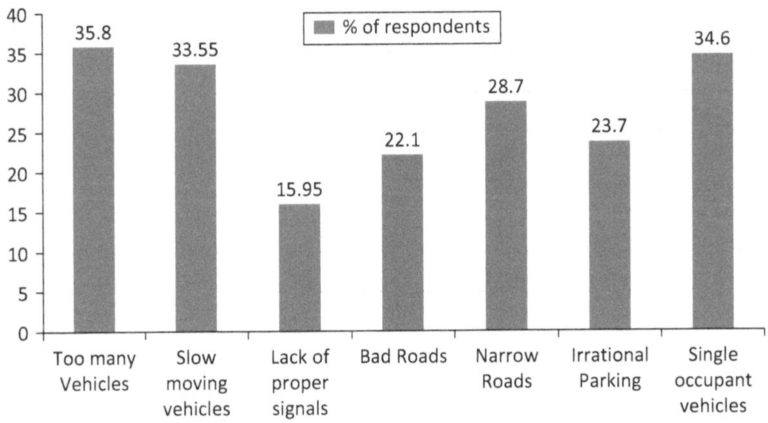

Figure 6.2 Causes of Traffic Congestion in Bengaluru (in %).

Source: Authors' Analysis Based on Primary Data.

Table 6.1 Bus ticket fares in different cities of India

Cities	*Fare for 5 kms (Rs.)*
Ahmedabad	8
Mumbai	14
Calcutta	8
Chandigarh	5
Delhi	10
Chennai	8
Pune	10
Bengaluru	15

Source: BBPV (Bengaluru Bus Prayanikara Vedika), 2019.

this, the study made a comparison of the bus ticket fares in other cities of the country provided in Table 6.1.

Among the major metro cities in the country, the bus fare in Bengaluru is comparatively high. This can be attributed to the nature of operation of public transport in the city. Though BMTC is a dominant public transport of the city, catering to the entire BBMP jurisdiction the corporation is under major problem. One such is, the entire revenue of the corporation is dependent on the ticket fare, leading to higher fare compared to other cities of the country. Further, we also elicited the opinion of respondents on the probable measures to reduce traffic congestion and improve the air quality in the city (Figure 6.3).

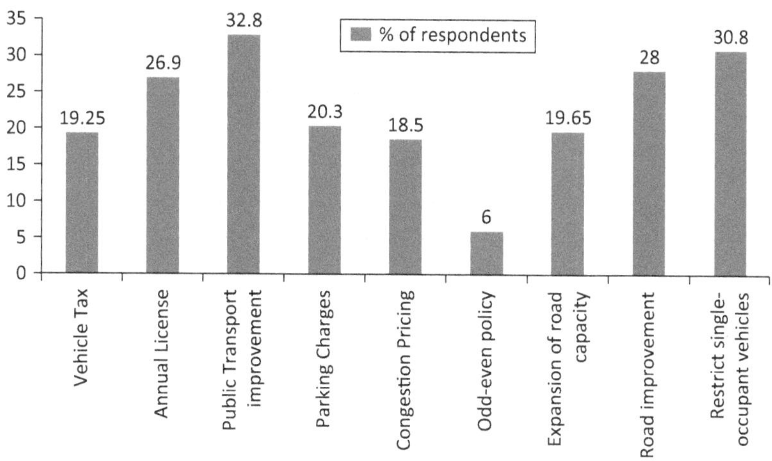

Figure 6.3 Measures to Reduce Traffic Congestion in Bengaluru.

Source: Authors' Analysis Based on Primary Data.

Majority of the respondents (32.8%) opined that enhancing the performance of public transport (frequency and accessibility) would reduce the congestion in the city to a larger extent. Restricting the single-occupant vehicles (30.8% responses) in the city centre is another preferred measure for decongesting the city. Even the policy of parking charges imposition is also preferred by the respondents who expected that there should be an improvement in the road quality (clearing potholes and bad reaches).

Another aspect of traffic congestion externalities is vehicular emissions which impairs public health. To improve the air quality from the vehicular emissions, the study elicited the opinion of the respondents on the measures to be implemented. Though certain congestion reduction measures also improve the air quality, apart from this, other measures are graphed in Figure 6.4. Among them, increasing the clean-fuel vehicles is considered to be an important measure for air quality improvement by the respondents. Around 27 per cent of the respondents opined that banning the old vehicles and planting more trees around the city would improve the air quality level.

The literature has extensive evidences on the policy instruments to internalize the traffic congestion externalities. Even our primary survey provided key insights on the preference of commuters regarding the viability of measures. The chapter will form the basis for deriving policy suggestions to any city. Based on these evidences, we have provided policy approach to Bengaluru city in Chapter 7.

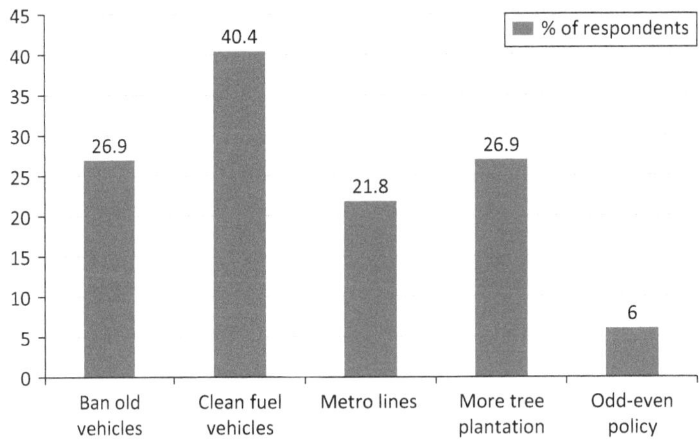

Figure 6.4 Measures to Improve the Air Quality in Bengaluru.

Source: Authors' Analysis Based on Primary Data.

6.6 Conclusion

The chapter has elaborated on the policy instruments and their effectives in handling the traffic congestion. Economists have long advocated road pricing as an optimal strategy to contain congestion, but it is observed that commuters in developing countries regard it as an additional tax burden. In the meantime, other alternative congestion control strategies are favoured, which may lead to sub-optimality. The alternative policies have their own merits and demerits. There is another possibility that the alternative measures may yield short-term relief to congestion, but these have proved less enduring in the long run. Policies such as road construction without accompanying vehicle restrictions may further exacerbate the congestion (Button & Verhoef, 1998). Based on Bengaluru's traffic situation, a mix of demand- and supply-side measures are offered (Chapter 7) to ease traffic congestion and improve the air quality in the city.

Note

1. AIR 1993 Ker 297 from www.indiankanoon.org.

References

Arnott, R., de Palma, A., & Lindsey, R. (1990). Economics of a bottleneck. *Journal of Urban Economics*, *27*, 11–30.

Arnott, R., de Palma, A., & Lindsey, R. (1994). Welfare effects of congestion tolls with heterogeneous commuters. *Journal of Transport Economics and Policy*, *28*, 139–162.

Baxbaum, N. J. (2009). Congestion pricing basics. https://transportation.ky.gov/congestion-toolbox/documents/congestion%20pricing%20basics.pdfto

BBMP Limits. http://bbmp.gov.in/pothole

BBPV (Bengaluru Bus Prayanikara Vedike). (2019). Why slashing bus fares is key to increasing BMTC's ridership. www.bengaluru.citizenmatters.in

Bhattacharjee, S., & Goetz, A. R. (2012). Impact of light rail on traffic congestion in Denver. *Journal of Transport Geography*, *22*(3), 262–270.

Button, K. J., & Verhoef, E. T. (Ed.). (1998). *Road pricing, traffic congestion and the environment, issues of efficiency and social feasibility*. Edward Elgar.

ECMT (European Conference of Ministers of Transport). (1999). Traffic congestion in Europe: Report of round table 110, European conference of ministers of transport, Paris, France. www.oecd-ilibrary.org

Button, K. J., & Costa, A. (1997). Economic efficiency gains from public transport regulatory changes in Europe. Paper to the 36th Western Regional Science Association Annual Conference, Hawaii.

Ewing, R., Hamidi, S., Gallican, F., Nelson, A. C., & Grace, J. M. (2014). Structural equation models of VMT growth in US urbanised areas. *Urban Studies*, *51*(14), 3079–3096. https://doi.org/10.1177/0042098013516521

Gillen, W. D. (1977). Estimation and specification of the effects of parking cost on urban transport mode choice. *Journal of Urban Economics*, *4*(2), 186–199.

Gomez, G. P. (1998). Environmental regulation: Uncertainty and threshold effects in the case of biodiversity. In M. Acutt & P. Mason (Eds.), *Environmental valuation, economic policy and sustainability: Recent advances in environmental economics*. Edward Elgar.

Gomez-Ibnez, J. A., & Small, K. A. (1994). *Road pricing for congestion management: A survey of international practice*. Transportation Research Board. National Academy Press.

Greenstone, M., Harish, S., Pande, R., & Sudarshan, A. (2017). The solvable challenge of air pollution in India. India Policy Forum 2017, July 11–12. www.ncaer.org

IIHS (Indian Institute for Human Settlements). (2015). Industrial policy and urban growth: IIHS RF Paper on Manufacturing cities. http://iihs.co.in/knowledge-gateway/wp-content

Jaffe, A. B., & Stavins, R. N. (1995). Dynamic incentives of environmental regulations: The effects of alternative policy instruments on technology diffusion. *Journal of Environment, Economics and Management*, *29*, 43–63.

Jeihani, M., et al. (2013). Development of a framework for transit-oriented development (TOD), Office of policy & research, Mayland State Highway Administration. http://tinyurl.com/mejjc84

Joseph, S. (1991). Traffic growth, the problems and solution. *Journal of Law and Society*, *18*, 26–134.

Kolstad, D. C. (2000). *Environmental economics*. Oxford University Press.

Litman, T. (2016). Smart congestion relief: Comprehensive evaluation of traffic congestion costs and congestion reduction strategies, Victoria transport policy institute. www.vtpi.org

Matsoukis, E. C. (1985). An assessment of vehicle restrains measures. *Transportation Quarterly*, *39*, 125–133.

Merugu, D., Prabhakar, S. B., & Rama, N. S. (2019). An incentive mechanism for decongesting the roads: A pilot program in Bangalore. www.web.stanford.edu

Mohring, H. (1989). The role of fuel taxes in controlling congestion. In World Bank Transport dept, *Transport policy, management and technology towards 2001*. Western Periodicals Company.

Mourato, S. (1998). Economic valuation in transition economies: An application of contingent valuation in Lake Balaton in Hungary. In M. Acutt & P. Mason (Eds.), *Environmental valuation, economic policy and sustainability: Recent advances in environmental economics*. Edward Elgar.

Nijakamp, P., & Shefer, D. (1998). *Urban transport externalities and pigouvian taxes: A network approach*. Edward Elgar Publishing.

OECD (Organization for Economic Co-Operation and Development). (1989). Environmental policy benefits: Monetary valuation. www.oecd.org

Panayotou, T. (1994). Economic instruments for environmental management and sustainable development. United Nations Environment Programme's consultative expert group meeting, Nairobi. Environmental Economics Series Paper no. 16. www.cbd.int/doc/nbsap/

Pigou, A. C. (1920). *Wealth and welfare*. Macmilan.

Shekar, S. (2015). Vehicular pollution in India: Laws and reactions. https://www.academia.edu/11723077/Vehicular_Pollution_In_India_Laws_and_Reactions

Sherman, R. (1972). Subsidies to relieve urban traffic congestion. *Journal of Transport Economics and Policy*, *6*, 22–31.

Small, A. K., & Gomez-Ibanez, J. A. (1998). Road pricing for congestion management: The transition from theory to policy. University of California Transportation Centre No. 391, 213–246.

Thomson, I. J. M. (1998). Reflections on the economics of traffic congestion. *Journal of Transport Economics and Policy*, *32*(1), 93–112.

TERI (The Energy and Resource Institute). (2010). Air quality assessment, emission inventory & source apportionment study of Bengaluru city. TERI.

Timilsina, R. G., & Dulal, B. H. (2009). Regulatory instruments to control environmental externalities from the transport sector. *European Transport*, *41*, 80–112.

UK Ministry of Transport. (1963). *Traffic in towns*. HMSO.

Vickrey, W. S. (1969). Congestion theory and transport investment. *American Economic Review*, *59*, 251–269.

Willson, R. W., & Shoup, D. C. (1990). Parking subsidies and travel choices: Assessing the evidence. *Transportation*, *17*(2), 141–157.

World Bank. (2018). Leveraging electric mobility for development and climate. Press release on December 4, 2018. https://www.worldbank.org/en/news/press-release

Chapter 7

Public Policy for Traffic Management

7.1 Introduction

From the previous chapter, we have established that traffic congestion is not a mere problem of infrastructure fallacy. It has a disastrous impact on the economy and environment. The book has clearly estimated the costs and its impacts. From the time loss cost to its health impacts, we have made estimations even to the intangible costs of traffic congestion. This is an important addition to the transport economic literature. In this chapter, we will highlight the major findings and its policy implications. Further, we have drafted a brief policy approach to Bengaluru city. This policy can be tailored to suit any metropolitan city which is facing similar traffic problems. The study has begun its analysis by understanding the nature and causes for the traffic problem. Using the time-series econometric analysis, we found that, economic concentration and economic growth in the form of increasing income levels and urbanization have a significant and positive impact on the personal vehicular growth in the country. This positive relationship is particularly evident in metropolitan cities due to their tremendous economic growth. However, these cities are facing a severe form of traffic congestion due to mismatch between vehicular growth and infrastructure network.

To prove this, the modal choice behaviour of the commuters is examined for Bengaluru city. The result indicated that there is a strong and positive preference in favour of private transport as against public transport. Similar findings are also observed in other metropolitan cities of the country. If this pattern continues, the cities of the country face severe traffic gridlock causing a huge economic loss. In this backdrop, the economic costs of traffic congestion for the city are estimated by classifying them into direct and indirect costs. An important contribution is made by highlighting the opportunity cost of time stuck in traffic congestion, rather than estimating the total travel time like other studies. The impact on environment is captured by the health implications of traffic-induced air pollution on commuters are quantified. For this, a causal relationship between the pollutant ($PM_{2.5}$) and its health impact (called dose–response function) is established using binary logit regression.

DOI: 10.4324/9781032662299-7

Using the cost of illness approach, the direct and indirect costs for the morbidity impacts are estimated. The mortality impacts of traffic congestion have been estimated using the contingent valuation method. To arrive at a viable policy measure, we examined the effectiveness of certain policy instruments to internalize the traffic congestion externalities.

7.2 Major Findings of the Study

The pace of economic growth and urbanization has a significant impact on the vehicular movement causing congestion. Though research studies have indicated that there traffic congestion is due to economic growth, our study has proved it empirically using time-series econometric tool for India. The result shows that there exists a positive long run cointegration among the variables. A 1 per cent increase in both PCI and urbanization would increase the personal vehicles by 0.38 and 0.36 per cent, respectively. This clearly brought out the severity of traffic congestion in India, which needs an urgent policy attention.

This further probed us to examine the situation of transport sector growth in metropolitan cities. By examining the five major metropolitan cities of India, it is highlighted that, among these cities, the vehicular growth in Bengaluru city is increasing at a faster rate. The city ranks second highest in terms of vehicular population in the country with 441 vehicles per 1,000 persons (next to New Delhi with 443 vehicles per 1,000 persons). Even in private vehicles, Bengaluru has the highest private motorization rate in the country. In contrast to this, the share of public transport in these cities is found decreasing. Hence, we are directed that Bengaluru not only signifies being the most dynamic city of the world, but sadly struggling to handle its traffic flow. Further, the literature is profound in pointing at the environmental impacts of traffic congestion. But there is no scientific and empirical evidence. In this regard, our study makes a key effort by conducting an econometric analysis on vehicular pollutant ($PM_{2.5}$) and vehicular growth. The results are quite interesting. We found a long-run relationship among the variables. This means, 1 per cent increase in the vehicular population and VKT would increase the $PM_{2.5}$ by 27 and 11 per cent, respectively. This infers that, as the number of vehicles increased (i.e. VKT), pollution also increases. An important finding from the analysis is related to metro ridership, where one unit increase in the ridership would reduce the $PM_{2.5}$ emissions by 30.9 per cent. This highlights that improving the public transportation will reduce the air pollution significantly.

Any travel-related studies are complete without understanding the modal choice. Even our study has examined it and analyzed by establishing the probability relation. Using multinomial logit regression, we infer that compared to female respondents, male respondents preferred private vehicles for their daily commute. Key factors like age, income, education, and traffic delay have positive probability on the modal-choice shift in favour of private transportation as against public transport. Further, the accessibility to public transportation is found to be a key factor determining the modal choice of the commuters. With these empirically profound results, we have estimated the economic costs of traffic congestion by classifying them into direct and indirect cost. The direct cost captures the time delay and fuel wastage cost, whereas the indirect cost estimates the productivity and health costs.

7.2.1 Direct Economic Cost of Traffic Congestion

Using the wage-rate approach, the time delay cost for the driver is estimated. On an average, the commuters in the city are stuck approximately 38 minutes every day in traffic congestion, which can be approximated as 7.3 days in a year. This would cause a time delay cost of Rs. 229 for every hour stuck in traffic congestion and an annual time loss of Rs. 40,668 per person. The total direct economic loss is estimated as Rs. 1.10 lakh per year. This is a significant loss to the economy.

The second component of the direct cost of traffic congestion is the fuel wastage cost. Approximately 59,796 litres of additional fuel are consumed by private vehicles which accounted for Rs. 45 lakhs in the study area. Instead of an ideal travel cost (fuel cost) of Rs. 17,335 per year (which forms 4.1% of PCI), the commuters in the city are incurring an additional fuel cost Rs. 16,618 due to traffic congestion (total travel cost of Rs. 33,953 every year). That means, the commuters are spending an almost 3.96 per cent of their per capita income unknowingly. This forms an implicit cost of traffic congestion.

The total direct cost of congestion (time and fuel loss) is estimated as Rs. 57,271 per year which is borne by the private vehicle commuter. This accounts for Rs. 1.55 crores. Further, among all the four zones, the costs incurred by the commuters in Zone 1 (CBD), is comparatively higher than other zones, indicating heavy traffic.

7.2.2 Indirect Economic Cost of Traffic Congestion

The indirect cost of congestion comprises of TDC on non-drivers and health and productivity costs. The non-drivers include public transport users who are the passive agents of traffic congestion. Every hour stuck in traffic congestion has a cost of Rs. 176 and every public transport user bear an annual additional cost of Rs. 27,796. This forms an annual TDC on non-drivers as approximately Rs. 40.21 lakhs.

The productivity loss is defined as the loss of productive (work) hour due to late arrivals, which a loss on the economy implicitly. From the primary survey, it is found that about 34 per cent of the commuters arrive late to the workplace, and they do not extend the workhour to compensate for the loss hours and hence cause productive hour loss. It is estimated that approximately Rs. 7.4 lakhs are being lost due to the late arrivals by the private vehicle users and around Rs. 4 lakhs by the public transport users, causing an aggregate loss of Rs. 11.4 lakhs to the city by losing 6,998 productive hours every year. The total indirect cost of congestion is estimated as on an average of Rs. 51.69 lakhs every year.

The total economic cost of traffic congestion is estimated as Rs. 2.06 crores per year. If this cost is approximated to the city (for the working population), the total economic cost of traffic congestion (excluding the health cost) would account approximately Rs. 245 billion, which is about 0.58 per cent of the City's GDP (2017–2018) being lost due to traffic congestion. Similar findings are found in CEBR (2014), TTI (2015) and many studies for developed countries.

Among the costs, the indirect cost is comparatively lesser (Rs. 27,796 of TDC) than the private vehicle (Rs. 57,271). It favours the investment in public transportation improvement which is more sustainable mobility mode. Even TDC on non-drivers is comparatively less in Zones 1 and 2 indicating the role of metro trains in handling the traffic congestion.

7.2.3 Health and Productivity Cost of Traffic Congestion

Another significant and often overlooked impact of traffic congestion is on the environment. The vehicular emissions are considered as the major source of outdoor air pollution in the urban areas. To account for this, the impact of vehicular emissions on human health is examined. With the help of the logistic regression, the dose–response function is established for the impact of traffic-related variables on respiratory infection. The result shows that, age, duration of travel, years of travel, and traffic exposure have a significant and positive impact on the respiratory-related illness due to traffic congestion (dependent variable). Key traffic-related variables namely, traffic exposure and $PM_{2.5}$ are found to cause 0.01 per cent and 2.5 per cent increase in the illness, respectively. An important finding is with respect to metro users, where the probability of illness would decrease by 5.5 per cent. This indicates the importance of mass transportation in improving the health and environment of the city. Further, we found that a commuter who travels more than 34 kms a day and is exposed to 43.5 minutes per day of traffic emissions, he/she is more likely to suffer from the issue of asthma. Similarly, 35 kms of travel and 42.7 minutes of exposure may lead to higher chances of respiratory infections.

The estimated the annual direct cost of illness (expenses towards medicines) due to traffic-related health issue is Rs. 4,944 per person. The absenteeism due to suffering from the traffic-related illnesses would cost an annual loss of Rs. 13,104 per person.

The total annual cost of illness is accounted for as Rs. 18,048 per person, which would form nearly 4.30 per cent of the per capita income of the sample. This shows the severity of traffic congestion on the commuter's health.

Using contingent valuation method, the estimated the mortality cost of traffic congestion due to prolonged illness. The willingness to pay responses are collected. The socio-economic variables like age, income and exposure contributed a significant and positive influence on the WTP responses except for gender. The travel and health variables like exposure, health treatment taken, and work-days loss also positively influence the WTP values. The result also recommends a modal shift towards public transport which will improve the health status of the commuters in the city. This would reduce the probability of travel-related illness 5.5 per cent and save almost Rs. 18,048 per person being lost due to health cost from traffic-related air pollution.

Using the risk factor of 0.018 per cent and value of risk for mortality reduction from the mean WTP, which is Rs. 1,60,552, the economic cost of mortality is estimated as Rs. 14.61 crores for 2018–2019 (based on OECD (2004) methodology). This is almost 0.03 per cent of the City's GDP (2018-2019) being lost due to the mortality attributable to traffic congestion emissions.

7.2.4 *Effectiveness of Economic Instruments of Traffic Congestion*

Road pricing is the most common and economically efficient measure advocated around the world. But it may have distributional impacts on the commuter and the economy. Hence, supporting the price mechanism is considered as a second-best policy measure particularly for the cities of developing countries.

Given these varied measures and their viabilities, we suggested for adopting hybrid instruments for decongesting and improving the air quality of the city. Based on our analysis from previous chapter, the policy measures are classified as demand and supply-side instruments. The supply-side measures include access management, parking restrictions, improving the road performance, and clean fuel programs. Under the demand-side management, improving the efficiency of public transportation in the city, establishing the annual license scheme, intelligent transport system, travel demand management, and bringing traffic awareness among the public are recommended.

7.3 Policy Recommendations to Ease Traffic Congestion for the Bengaluru city

The sustainable development goals urge for safer and efficient modes in transportation assuring equality and efficiency. Additionally, the forum also argues to curb air pollution, especially in urban space (Ian & Walls, 2007).

Table 7.1 Policy measures for Bengaluru city

Supply-side policies	*Demand-side policies*
• Access management: CBD entry restriction, HV restriction • Parking management: permit based parking or parking charges in CBD, parking restrictions. • Improving road performance: proper signals with yellow light indication; repairing road (Potholes & Bad reaches) • Clean fuel program; catalytic converter	• Efficiency of public transportation: frequency of bus and reduced fare for both bus and metro; Dedicated bus lanes • Annual License Scheme • Intelligent Transport System (ITS) • Travel Demand Management (TDS) • Education

Source: Census, 2011.

This will induce to frame policy instruments carefully to suit the needs of the spatio-temporal conditions of the area. In this line, a policy draft is prepared based on the analysis.

The opportunity cost of time delay (TDC) forms a significant part of the total traffic congestion cost. To reduce this, the city requires a comprehensive policy which incorporates both CAC and economic instruments. This hybrid policy intends for a modal shift, which would decongest the city and improve the air quality.

7.3.1 Supply-side Measures to Ease Traffic Congestion

Access Management: As the traffic congestion is found to be severe in the CBD of the city, a physical restriction of the private vehicles in this zone may be a viable policy. Under access management, the city can restrict the entry of single-occupant vehicles to the city centre (CBD). Further, it has been already mandated to restrict the entry of heavy vehicles (HV) to the centre during peak hours. This measure should be implemented with proper surveillance. This measure is supported by nearly 30.8 per cent of commuter in this city.

Parking Management: Free and irrational parking has been an issue in traffic management for the city's traffic department. The on-street parking needs to be regulated. Nearly 20.3 per cent of commuter in the city supported the introduction of parking charge system in the city. Hence, we recommend that the city can adopt parking permit or charge.

Improving Road Performance: Being the supply-side measure, this policy does not advocate the increase in road capacity, rather it suggests for the betterment of the existing roads by repairing the potholes and bad reaches. It is estimated that there are around 5,630 potholes and 12,926 kms of bad reaches extending up to 1865.5 kms on the city roads, which is slowing down the traffic-flow in the city (BBMP, 2019). Rather than investing in creating more road capacity, measures should be undertaken to make the existing road viable. Another aspect of road performance includes traffic-signal management. It is observed from the primary survey that out of 15 study junctions, around 13 junctions lack proper traffic-signal timer mechanism. This refers to the indication of yellow light in the signals which indicate the traffic flow to stop and timer in the signal which indicate the drivers to turn-off their engines. Providing such mechanisms not only ease the traffic movement in the city but also reduce the fuel wastages to a large extent.

Clean Fuel Program: As an emission reduction policy, the commuters should be encouraged for adopting the clean fuel vehicles like electric, CNG, or Lithium. Though these measures are not aimed at decongesting the city but might improve the air quality in the city. Another important strategy which has been in practice is to adopt catalytic converters. It can be mandated to use three-way catalytic converters in all vehicles to reduce emissions. Further, clean fuel program should also initiate mandatory PUC (Pollution Under Control) sticker to the vehicles. Vehicle maintenance and inspections would long way in reduction of the vehicular emissions. The program also includes the implementation of BS-VI norms in the city by 2020.

Demand-side Measures to Ease Traffic Congestion

The demand-side policies aim at changing the travel behaviour of the individuals. It has been argued by Sharp (1967) that, the measure to relieve traffic congestion in urban areas should shift of private commuting pattern to public transport. The shift from car-to-bus requires state intervention (Sharp, 1967) in the form of taxation, parking policies, or direct restriction of private cars.

Shift to Public Transportation: The shift requires an incentive mechanism which could make the public transport more attractive. As an initial step, a reduction in the ticket fare of BMTC will attract commutes from private vehicles. This measure should also be supported by subsequent increase in the number of buses and completion of metro train phases. The number of buses in the city is around 6,632 (BMTC report, 2017–2018). Based on the global norm on public transport provision (UITP, 2014), which requires 120 buses per one lakh population buses, the city needs to have around 15,486 buses. This indicates a difference of around 8854 buses needs to be introduced in the city. From the efficiency perspective, there is a need to increase the frequency of buses. The adoption of a dedicated bus-lane with proper traffic management in the CBD can ease the traffic congestion in the zone.

Annual License Scheme: Studies have advocated that the implementation of road pricing creates distributional impacts. As an alternative to pricing, the city can implement the annual license scheme for private vehicle users. The scheme requires acquiring a license to drive any private vehicle in the city, which should be renewed every year. This license should be linked to the driving license of the commuters. The major advantage of this system is the administration and transaction costs are kept relatively low.

The city is inflicting a huge influx of private vehicles. This is imposing an economic cost which forms nearly 0.69 per cent of city's GDP. To reduce this, the implementation of an annual license fee for private vehicles can be recommended. This would not only generate revenue to the department of traffic police but also induce people to shift to public transport. The license fee can be fixed based on the economic loss for each modal type (estimated in the study) and on the VKT of the vehicle. For instance, a two-wheeler user can be imposed first phase annual license fees of Rs. 1,146 (10% of the FWC) and car user with Rs. 3,218 and gradual increase by 10 per cent every year or the license amount can be positively varied based on the VKT of the vehicle. The amount collected should be diverted to subsidize the ticket fare in BMTC and metro train.

Travel Demand Management (TDM): As productive hour loss due to traffic congestion is high in the city, it requires an effective implementation of traffic demand management. This calls for an active participation from private companies (MNCs) to incentivize their employees to use public transport and avoid drive-alone. This measure should be supported by restricted the parking facility by implementing the pay and park system. These companies can also be given fiscal incentives for adopting clean-fuel vehicles for their transportation by the government. Additionally, the companies can also adopt work-from-home options (where-ever possible) to reduce the mobility of employees, which eases traffic congestion in the city.

Traffic management system (TMS): The traffic management system includes improvement in the reliability of the traffic signals with a timer and yellow-light indication. As nearly 4 per cent of PCI of forms the fuel wastage cost due to traffic congestion, improving the traffic management in the city will reduce this cost significantly.

Intelligent Transport System (ITS): This includes improved travel information with real-time traffic-flow information and signs of congestion that allow travellers to anticipate, avoid, and respond to the delays. Improving transit information may also shift the potential drivers to public transit. To reduce the health cost and improve the air quality, the BTP can initiate the strict implementation of emission compliance by all the vehicles in the city. This requires the compulsory checking of the PUC certificate of the vehicles by the traffic department. In addition to this, the study recommends the installation of three-way catalytic converters in all the vehicles. This improves fuel efficiency and reduces emissions.

Education: Educating the public regarding the ill-effects of traffic congestion, especially the health cost, would go a long way in reducing the congestion. This strategy is workable only if the other policies are implemented successfully. For example, educating people to shift to public transport is only possible if the efficiency of the public transport system is improved.

The policy recommended so far based on the estimate can help other metropolitan cities to analyze their traffic situation and adopt suitable policies.

7.4 Conclusion

Our study made an innovative approach to account for the economic cost of traffic congestion. These costs have accounted for both implicit and explicit costs. The book has employed standard and scientific methods for arriving at its results. These results form the basis for the policy makers in arriving at sustainable transport policies. Even though the study arrived at the inclusive results, there can be further works which would provide deeper insights into the problem. For instance, instead of working commuters, the future study can incorporate larger sample to know the impact by employing the similar methodology. Further, this book exclusively deals with the health implications of traffic congestion on commuters. This can be extended to other set of people in the society. To this level, our estimate provides the lower bounds of traffic congestion costs. But these estimates can act as benchmark costs to the policy makers and guide them to employ viable and sustainable transport policies, which would aim at reduction of these costs. In similar line, the book provides a guideline in terms of framework, methodology and analysis in deriving traffic congestion costs to other researchers. The book stands one of its kind in considering traffic congestion as an economic problem and estimating its externality cost.

References

BBMP (Bruhat Bengaluru Mahanagara Palike). (2019). Status of potholes/roadpertaining to BBMP limits. Retrieved from http://bbmp.gov.in/pothole

CEBR (Centre for Economics and Business Research). (2014). The future economic and environmental cost of gridlock in 2030: An assessment of the direct and indirect economic and environmental cost of idling in road traffic congestion to households in the UK, France, Germany & USA. CEBR.

Ian, W. H. P., & Walls, H. M. (2007). Automobile externalities and policies. *Journal of Economic Literature*, *XLV*, 373–399.

OECD (Organisation for Economic Co-operation and Development). (2004). Project on decoupling transport impacts and economic growth: *Analysis of the links between transport and economic growth*. ENV/EPOC/WPNEP/T(2003)4/FINAL: OECD.

Sharp, C. H. (1967). The choice between cars and buses on urban roads. *Journal of Transport Economics and Policy*, *1*(1), 104–111.

Texas Transportation Institute (TTI). (2015). Urban mobility report. http://mobility.tamu.edu/ums

UITP (International Association of Public Transport). (2014). A bright future in store for the bus. www.utip.org

Appendix

Appendix 2A

Table 2.1
Figure 2.2A
The straight lines represent critical bounds at 5 per cent significance level.

Appendix 3A

Table 3.1A
Figure 3.1A
The straight line represents critical bounds at 5 per cent significance level.

Table 2.1A Diagnostic test result on PCI and vehicular growth

LM test	*BP test*	*Jarque-bera*
0.32 (0.72)	1.08 (0.40)	0.61 (0.28)

Parenthesis is the probability values.

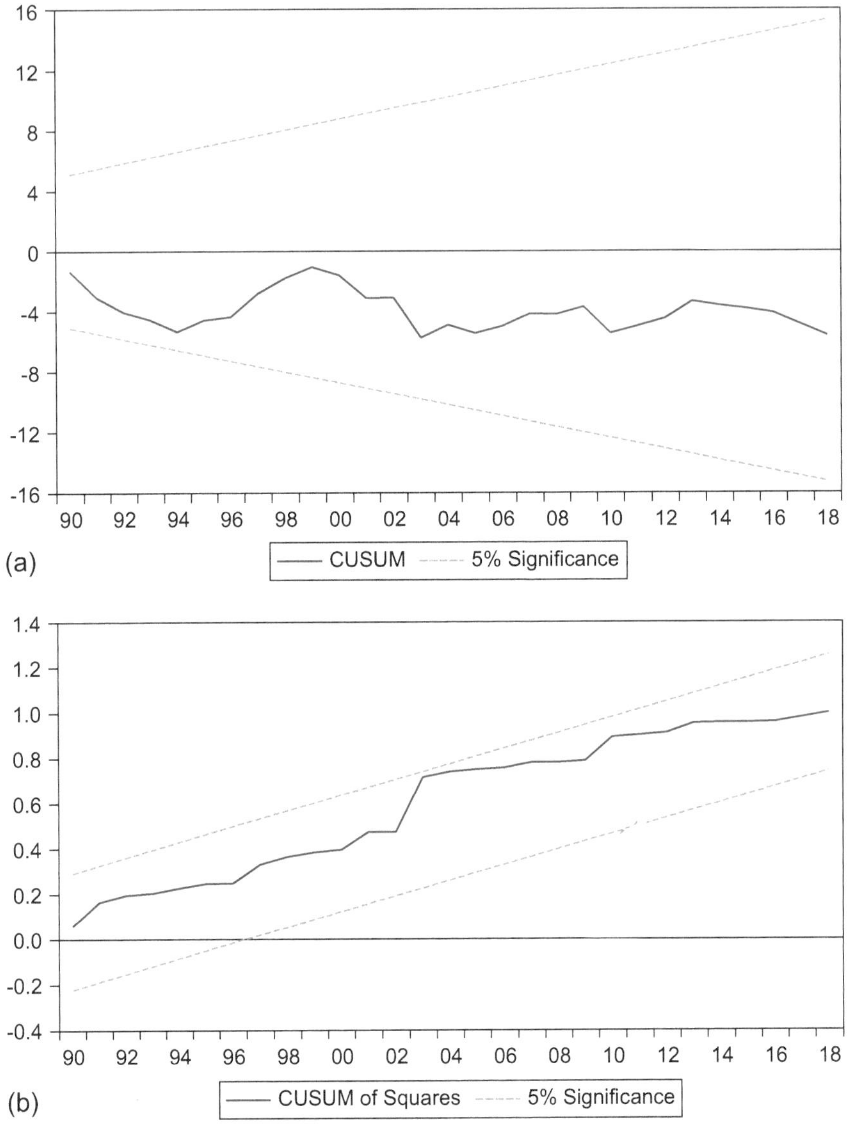

Figure 2.2A CUSUM Test and CUSUM of Squares Test of ARDL model on (a) PCI and (b) vehicular Growth.

Table 3.1A Diagnostic test result of ARDL model on vehicular growth and $PM_{2.5}$

LM test	*BP test*	*Jarque-bera*
0.80 (0.45)	0.45 (0.6)	0.71 (0.39)

Parenthesis is the probability values.

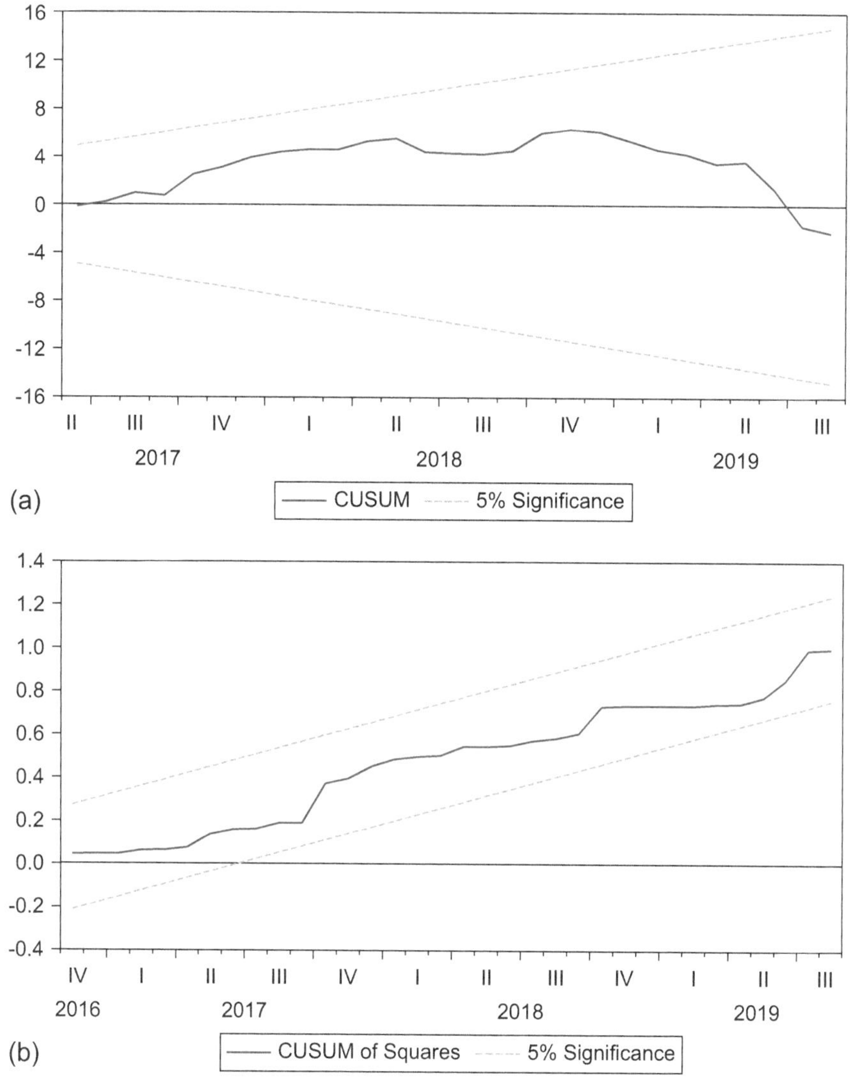

Figure 3.1A CUSUM Test and CUSUM of Squares Test of ARDL Model on Vehicular Growth and $PM_{2.5}$.

Index

Note: The numbers in **bold** represents tables and numbers in *italics* represents figures.

FSC
www.fsc.org
MIX
Papier | Fördert
gute Waldnutzung
FSC® C083411

Kolibri 360 GmbH
Ferdinand-Jühlke-Straße 7
99095 Erfurt, Deutschland
produktsicherheit@kolibri360.de